Peter G. Ahr
'72

ACCORDING TO JOHN

BOOKS BY ARCHIBALD M. HUNTER
Published by *The Westminster Press*

According to John

The Gospel According to St Paul
(A Revised Edition of *Interpreting Paul's Gospel*)

Teaching and Preaching the New Testament

Paul and His Predecessors

Interpreting the Parables

Introducing the New Testament

Introducing New Testament Theology

Interpreting the New Testament, 1900–1950

The Work and Words of Jesus

The Message of the New Testament

According to *JOHN*

The New Look at the Fourth Gospel

by ARCHIBALD M. HUNTER

THE WESTMINSTER PRESS · PHILADELPHIA

Scripture quotations from the Revised Standard Version of the Bible are copyright, 1946 and 1952, by the Division of Christian Education of the National Council of Churches, and are used by permission.

Standard Book No. 664–24850–0
Library of Congress Catalog Card No. 69–14199

Published by the Westminster Press ®
Philadelphia, Pennsylvania

Printed in the United States of America

CONTENTS

ABBREVIATIONS

A.B.S.J.	R. E. Brown, *The Gospel according to St John*, I-XII (Anchor Bible Commentary)
B.J.R.L.	*The Bulletin of the John Rylands Library*
E.T.	*Expository Times*
H.T.F.G.	C. H. Dodd, *Historical Tradition in the Fourth Gospel*
I.F.G.	C. H. Dodd, *The Interpretation of the Fourth Gospel*
J.B.L.	*The Journal of Biblical Literature*
LXX	Septuagint
NEB	*New English Bible*
N.T.S.	*New Testament Studies*
RSV	*Revised Standard Version of the Bible*
S.J.T.	*The Scottish Journal of Theology*
T.L.Z.	*Theologische Literaturzeitung*
T.W.N.T.	*Theologisches Wörterbuch zum Neuen Testament*
Z.Th.K.	*Zeitschrift für Theologie und Kirche*
Z.N.W.	*Zeitschrift für die neutestamentliche Wissenschaft*

1

St John's Gospel Today

I

O F the making of books on the Gospel of St John there seems to be no end. Each succeeding decade brings its fresh harvest, so that the ordinary student, anxious to keep himself up to date, finds himself 'faint yet pursuing' in the professors' wake. But (the cynical may ask) do all these books and articles really increase our understanding of 'the spiritual Gospel', or are the savants but ringing the changes on old problems and darkening counsel for the plain man with their learned words?

We believe it beyond question that the Johannine debate has, in recent years, taken some remarkable and encouraging turns, and that it is not untrue to speak, as the Bishop of Woolwich has done, of a 'new look' coming over the fourth gospel.

Before going further, it will be well to pick out, with a word of comment, some of the highlights or landmarks, of Johannine study in the last thirty years.

In 1938 P. Gardner-Smith of Cambridge successfully re-opened the whole question of the dependence of John on the synoptics. In three words, he denied dependence.

In 1939 Eduard Schweizer of Basel, by using a carefully selected set of Johannine criteria,[1] showed that the gospel reveals practically everywhere the same linguistic characteristics, and so struck a powerful blow for its unity.

In 1940, there appeared, posthumously, E. C. Hoskyns' truly 'theological' commentary on the gospel. St John, he argued, brings out the wholeness lying hidden in the synoptic narratives and sayings; he sees the Story of Jesus *sub specie aeternitatis;* and his theme is 'the non-historical which makes sense of history'.

In 1941 Rudolf Bultmann of Marburg published his *Kommentar* which not only had something new to say about the gospel's sources and its Gnostic background, but elucidated John's theology in characteristically existential ways.

In 1950 K. G. Kuhn of Heidelberg first drew attention to the importance of the Dead Sea Scrolls for illuminating the background of the gospel.

In 1953 C. H. Dodd of Cambridge brought out his *Interpretation of the Fourth Gospel* which shed much light on the background, key-words, structure and meaning of the gospel.

In 1955 there appeared from the pen of C. K. Barrett of Durham the first full-scale English commentary based on the Greek text since Bernard's.

In 1956 Victor Martin of Geneva published a very important early MS of the gospel recovered from the sands of Egypt—Bodmer Papyrus II, or P66.[2]

In 1963 C. H. Dodd followed up his first book with an equally important one on (as the book's title has it) 'Historical tradition in the Fourth Gospel'.

In 1966 Raymond Brown of Baltimore, a learned and liberal Roman Catholic scholar, produced the first of his two *Anchor Bible* volumes on John's gospel and epistles, in which he successfully harvested the findings of many scholars, Protestant as well as Catholic, and gave us his own lucid and admirable exposition of the gospel, chapters 1-12.

Perhaps the most important consequence of all this scholarly labour has been the new emphasis on the historical worth of John's gospel. This is a matter we shall keep steadily in view. Meantime it may be enough to contrast the verdicts of two eminent scholars. Writing about thirty years ago Kirsopp Lake declared,[3] 'John may contain a few fragments of true tradition, but in the main it is fiction.' (This is the kind of judgment one normally hears passed on the apocryphal gospels.) Writing in 1963, C. H. Dodd[4] concluded: 'Behind the Fourth Gospel lies an ancient tradition independent of the other Gospels and meriting serious consideration as a contribution to our knowledge of the historical facts concerning Jesus Christ.'

Clearly, even when we have made allowance for the different temperaments of the two scholars quoted, significant progress must have been made in the thirty intervening years of Johannine study to justify a verdict like Dodd's. What shapes and directions, then, has it been taking?

Let us look back for a moment. Near the beginning of the century quite different questions seemed to occupy the scholars' attention. For some the quest was for a hypothetical *Grundschrift*, or basic document, thought to underlie the additions of various later editors. Others were convinced that the gospel as we now have it had got out of its original order and that some skilful reshuffling of its chapters would lay bare the gospel's order which John intended. (Let the reader turn up John's gospel in Moffatt's translation (1913), and he will see Moffatt switching chapters about in order to get back to the original order. Moffatt was only one of many re-arrangers.)

Nowadays, however, *Grundschriften* have gone right out of fashion, and fewer and fewer scholars undertake to put the gospel back into its right order. (To be sceptical of such re-arranging is not to deny the possibility of accidental displacements in a parent manuscript of the gospel, nor is it to deny that sometimes re-arrangements apparently improve the sense and connexion.) Thus, if we reverse the order of John, chapters 5 and 6, we seem to improve the geography of Jesus' movements. Yet all such re-arranging implies that we *know* the order John intended—a pretty big assumption. We must not confuse 'feelings' with 'proof'; and it is significant that most of our recent commentators—Hoskyns, Dodd, Barrett, Lightfoot, *et al.*—do no re-arranging.

The story then is of the abandonment of old quests and of the undertaking of new ones which promise to take the fourth gospel out of its isolation and restore it to favour in the scholars' sight. (The parish priest and the straightforward layman, as Hoskyns observed, have never doubted its spiritual value.) What factors have influenced this new trend? Some are textual, some linguistic, some archaeological, some documentary, and so on. It will help the reader if right at the outset we indicate some of them briefly.

II

Let us start with the text. It is a fact that we now possess more papyrus copies of John—17 in all—than of any other New Testament book. Among them perhaps the three most interesting are P52, P66 and P75.

The scrap of papyrus now called P52, preserved in the Rylands Library, Manchester, contains only five verses of John 18. It was published in 1935. Since, in the experts' opinion, it belongs to the first half of the second century, it ranks as the oldest NT MS we have. It proves that the gospel was circulating in Egypt, say, about A.D. 130 and must—if we allow a generation for the book to travel from Ephesus—have been written not later than A.D. 100. Here is a *terminus ad quem* for the date of the gospel.

P66, or Bodmer Papyrus II, published in 1956, contains most of John[5] and is dated about A.D. 200. It is thus about a hundred and fifty years earlier than Codex Vaticanus and Codex Sinaiticus.

P75, Bodmer Papyrus XV, published in 1961, does not preserve nearly so much of the gospel[6] as P66, but its date is approximately the same.

These two MSS are full of textual interest, and when they agree they provide very strong evidence for a reading.

Thus, in the last thirty years, the recovery of papyrus MSS from the sands of Egypt has not only helped with the dating of the gospel but made us surer that we possess its original text.

From text we turn to language. The story here might be entitled 'From Burney to Black', to name the two scholars who span a generation in which the gospel's Greek has been studied in order to decide the question: Is the gospel a straight translation from an Aramaic original, or does the evidence suggest a man writing in Greek whose mother-tongue was Aramaic? In the early 'twenties C. F. Burney of Oxford (supported by Torrey of Yale) learnedly argued the first view. He did not convince his critics. If the gospel were a translation from the Aramaic, we should have expected the Aramaisms to be distributed more or less evenly throughout it. In fact, there are sections, mostly narrative, which are innocent of them. Matthew Black represents the modern and probable view, viz. that, though John wrote in Greek, he was an Aramaic speaker.

From linguistic studies let us move on to archaeological discoveries which have helped, in recent years, to shape the new look on the gospel.

Time was when it was fashionable among advanced scholars to take a poor view of John's topography, to suggest that he really had no accurate knowledge of the terrain, towns and sites he mentions in his gospel, to conclude that his details of locality were not to be trusted.

In the last thirty years the spade of the archaeologist has dealt some hard knocks to this scepticism. Let us content ourselves here with only two examples: (1) The century-long question mark over the Pool of Bethesda has now been removed for ever. Excavations begun in the nineteenth century and completed in the 'thirties of this one have laid bare the long-lost Pool and vindicated the almost guide-book accuracy of John 5.1 'Now there is in Jerusalem by the sheep gate a pool, called in Hebrew Bethesda, which has five porticoes.' (ii) Where were Pilate's headquarters when he sat in judgment on Jesus? Where, in fact, was 'the place called The Pavement, and in Hebrew, Gabbatha' (19.13)? Though tradition had placed 'Pilate's House' near the Antonia Fort in the north-west corner of the Temple area, for a long time good scholars believed Pilate had his headquarters in Herod's palace on the high western hill. Now, thanks to the researches of L. H. Vincent in the 'thirties, tradition has been confirmed. The Pavement can be seen and walked on.

But the best-known archaeological event of our time with a bearing on John's gospel was undoubtedly the finding in 1947 of the Dead Sea scrolls. This shed new light on John's conceptual background. Every student of the gospel knows that John likes to traffic in antitheses like light and darkness, truth and error, life and death. This is the language of dualism. But of what kind? Before the scrolls were discovered, scholars identified it with the Greek and metaphysical dualism of 'classical' Gnosticism, known to us from the writings of the church fathers (and now to be seen in the Gnostic documents found in 1946 at Chenoboskion). When, however, the scrolls were studied, K. G. Kuhn, W. F. Albright and others quickly saw that the Johannine antitheses and dualism found their best parallels in the Qumran documents. In both John and the scrolls the dualism was not metaphysical but ethical and eschatological. Not surprisingly Kuhn announced that we had now found 'the native soil' of the Fourth Gospel in southern Palestine.

Doubtless, in the 'first fine careless rapture' of discovery, the researchers over-stated their claim, exposing themselves to the charge of 'Scrollomania'. It would be foolish to tell anyone, 'If you want to find the spiritual background of the fourth gospel, all you need to study is the scrolls.' Behind both John and the scrolls stand the Old Testament and Palestinian Judaism, rabbinical as well as 'non-conformist'; and it is well to remember that in the Judaism of New Testament times there was a strong Greek strain. Nevertheless, when we have uttered this caveat, there remains much truth in the claim of Millar Burrows[7] that 'we do not need to look outside Palestinian Judaism for the soil in which Johannine theology grew'.

We turn finally to the question of gospel documents and John's dependence on them. Did he know and use the synoptic gospels?

When Canon Streeter of Oxford published his famous *The Four Gospels* in 1925, there was a general consensus among the critics that John knew and used Mark and probably Luke (some would have added Matthew). In 1938, as we have noted, Gardner-Smith denied all dependence, thus inaugurating a debate which has gone on ever since. For a while some of our leading scholars were unpersuaded by his arguments, and indeed in the 'fifties the commentaries of Barrett and Lightfoot were found still supporting Streeter. Earlier in Germany Bultmann found the case for John's dependence unproved—he had his own theory of the gospel's sources.[8] In this country the Johannine expert W. F. Howard, before his death, confessed himself a convert to the new view. In 1954 the Danish scholar Bent Noack championed the case for oral tradition against all theories of literary dependence. And in 1963 C. H. Dodd, who had earlier agreed with Streeter, published his massive *Historical Tradition in the Fourth Gospel*, which was one long and impressive argument to show not only that John was independent of the synoptics but had at his disposal a very early and Palestinian oral tradition about Jesus. Three years later Raymond Brown declared his general support for Dodd.

In short, in 1938 Gardner-Smith's was a lone voice protesting John's independence; in 1968 his view may almost be said to represent 'critical orthodoxy'. If it is true, as we believe it is, it has important consequences for the whole Johannine debate.

III

We have mentioned some of the current trends and issues in Johannine studies, and tried to show how they affect our understanding of the gospel.

Among those who have led the way in the new approach is the present Bishop of Woolwich, now world-famous as an *avant garde* theologian, but before his elevation to the episcopate known to the scholarly world as a fine New Testament scholar. It was at the Oxford Conference on the Four Gospels in 1957 that he read his paper with the title 'The New Look on the Fourth Gospel', later published in *Twelve New Testament Studies*.[9] In this essay he covers some of the same ground as we have been covering; but he also raises some bigger theological points in such a challenging way that we make no apology for summarizing here his contrast between 'the old look' and 'the new look' on the gospel. It will serve to set the stage for some of our ensuing chapters.

By 'the old look' on the fourth gospel Dr J. A. T. Robinson (as he then was) meant that which prevailed among more radical scholars in the early decades of the century, and which still figures in some textbooks. He summed it up under five heads:

1. John knew and used the synoptics.
2. He wrote in Ephesus, among Greeks and Gnostics, about the end of the first century or later.
3. He was essentially a witness to the Christ of faith, not to the Jesus of history.
4. He represented the end term in the evolution of New Testament theology.
5. He was not himself an eye-witness, nor an apostle.

These five opinions represented the critical orthodoxy of that time, and their cumulative effect was to set John at one or more removes from the events he records and so to minimize the worth of his testimony to the Jesus of history.

To these Robinson opposed five features—'straws in the wind, all blowing in the same direction'—of the new look he saw coming over the gospel in recent study:

First: an ever-growing number of scholars now deny John's dependence on the synoptics. If John preserves independent and early tradition, he must be, potentially at least, as near as the synoptics to the historical truth about Jesus.

Second: the evidence of the scrolls shows that for John's essential background we do not need to go beyond southern Palestine in the years between the Crucifixion and the Fall of Jerusalem, i.e. between A.D. 30 and 70.

Third: these two considerations have inevitably modified the critics' third opinion—that John is not a reliable witness to the Jesus of history. Of course he is a witness to the Christ of faith; but so also are the synoptics. What distinguishes the new look is a readiness to recognize that in John we may often be as near to the Jesus of history as in the synoptics and, sometimes, nearer.

Fourth: the old critical orthodoxy saw John as the end term of the theological development of the New Testament: that is, he stood, so to speak, on the shoulders of great predecessors like Paul. But is this really so?[10] What evidence is there that John was a spiritual disciple of Paul's? There is much evidence against it. True, John is a mature theological thinker. But does maturity necessarily imply lateness? Paul was a pretty mature theologian by the year A.D. 60. May not John's theological thinking also have matured earlier than we suppose?

Fifth: If the old argument for the apostolic authority of the gospel (classically stated by Westcott) is no longer tenable, it can be re-stated in an acceptable modern form, viz. in terms of the earliness and trustworthiness of the historical tradition embedded in St John. The gospel claims to embody eye-witness testimony; and what the defenders of 'the new look' on the gospel undertake is to trace John's tradition back to the earliest days 'not through the memory of one old man but through the ongoing life of a community'. The result is to give us a confidence in the gospel as a historical source quite inconceivable fifty years ago.

To the question whether we can eliminate the 'one old man' from any discussion of the gospel's apostolic authority we shall come back later. Meanwhile it will be agreed that Robinson's theses admirably prepare the way for our more detailed discussion.

After a short chapter on the style and language of the gospel, we shall discuss its background, especially as it has been illuminated by the scrolls. Next, we shall consider the gospel tradition of St John and his topography, before going on to study the course of Jesus' ministry in the fourth gospel, and the place and purpose of miracles in it. A chapter on the parables in St John will pave the way for a study of the words of Jesus in the Johannine idiom. And we shall round off our discussion by considering the apostolic authority of the gospel and adding some pages on the abiding worth and relevance of the gospel.

NOTES

[1] Schweizer's book was called *EGO EIMI*. By Johannine criteria are meant phrases like 'on the last day', 'lay down one's life', 'of himself', besides features like epexegetic *hina* and a doubled 'amen' before a saying of Jesus.

[2] W. M. Bodmer, a Swiss bibliophile who founded the Bodmer library.

[3] In the *Albert Schweitzer Jubilee Book*, p. 431.

[4] *H.T.F.G.*, p. 423.

[5] Chapters 1-14 plus fragments of the remaining chapters.

[6] John 1-4 and 8-9 plus portions of 5-7 and 10-13.

[7] *The Dead Sea Scrolls*, p. 340.

[8] Bultmann believed that by style-criticism he had discovered three written sources behind John: (1) a collection of Discourses, Gnostic in origin and probably translated from Aramaic; (2) a 'signs' source; and (3) another source, independent of the synoptics which supplied John's Passion Story etc. Bultmann's source-theory has not survived criticism. Says P. Parker, 'It looks as though, if St John used written sources, he wrote them all himself' (*J.B.L.*, LXXV (1956), 304).

[9] *Studies in Biblical Theology* No. 34, 1962.

[10] The view that John's theology depends on Paul's, Théo Preiss (*Life in Christ*, p. 12f.) calls 'a by-product of that vast Hegelian mythology which insisted on tracing the evolution of Christianity in an unilinear way. Since John wrote after Paul, he must at all costs stem from him.'

2

The Language of St John

AMONG the evangelists St John writes a style all his own. It is not, by classical canons, good Greek, yet it is clear, individual and strangely impressive Greek. St John uses a small vocabulary, builds his sentences simply, is sparing of adjectives, and likes the perfect tense. Among his idiosyncrasies are a fondness for combining the positive and negative sides of the same thing ('he confessed and denied not') and a liking for short dramatic sentences ('Jesus wept.' 'And it was night.' 'Now Barabbas was a robber.'). But the dominant notes of his style are simplicity and grandeur. What Arnold said of Wordsworth (who was a lover of this gospel) we may say of John: 'the expression may be bald, but it is bald as the bare moun-tain-tops are bare—with a baldness full of grandeur.' 'Never in my life,' testified Luther, 'have I read a book written in simpler words, and yet the words are inexpressible.' 'Incapable of writing a paragraph in acceptable Greek,' said Théo Preiss,[1] 'St John plays on his two manuals with equal ease and mastery. He evokes the image of Jesus in the most humble and most splendid features.'

But, having said this, we have not yet raised the question which is of special interest for our enquiry: Is John's Greek just typical *Koine* vernacular Greek of the first century A.D.—the kind of Greek we find in the more literate papyri which archaeologists have, for almost a century now, been digging up from the sands of Upper Egypt? Or does John's Greek betray an unmistakable Aramaic idiom—as, in the high-priest's courtyard, Peter's 'north-country' accent betrayed his Galilean origin (Matt. 26.73 'Your accent gives you away' NEB)?

Let us summarize a long debate.[2] Towards the end of the last century Bishop Lightfoot[3] pronounced John's gospel 'perhaps the most Hebraic book in the New Testament'. But, at the beginning of this one, when the discovery of the papyri seemed to have exploded the belief that New Testament Greek was something *sui generis*—'the language of the Holy Ghost' as Richard Rothe had put it in 1863—Adolf Deissmann vigorously contended that John's was simply vernacular Greek, and in this country J. H. Moulton agreed, 'John's style is not Semitic'.

Meantime, however, in Oxford the noted Semitist C. F. Burney was coming to a very different conclusion, and in 1922, with his book *The Aramaic Origin of the Fourth Gospel*, 'he threw horse, foot and artillery into the fray' against Deissmann and his supporters. To prove the Aramaic origin of John's gospel, Burney piled one linguistic argument upon another: in sentence-structure, conjunctions, pronouns, verbs and negatives he found evidence for his theory; and, in order to clinch his point, he produced examples of alleged mistranslation from an underlying Aramaic. C. C. Torrey quickly rallied to his support and even out-Burneyed Burney. Not John alone but all four gospels (he said) were translations from Aramaic originals, and he had his own collection of mistranslations to prove his case.

Since then the experts have spent much time sifting their evidence, and it now appears, as so often happens, that the truth lies somewhere in the middle, between Burney and Deissmann. John's gospel is not a straight translation from the Aramaic original but there are sufficient Semitisms—Jewish idioms, Hebrew and Aramaic, glimmering through John's Hellenistic Greek—to warrant the belief that his mother-tongue was Aramaic, or that the traditions about Jesus which he preserves were Aramaic in origin.

II

To begin with, a number of Aramaic words appear in transliteration in John's gospel, often with an added explanation, presumably for the benefit of non-Semitic readers: Cephas, Messias, Siloam, Thomas, Gabbatha, Golgotha, rabbouni.

Next, we find in his gospel what is called *parataxis*, i.e. the co-ordination of sentences by 'and' instead of using (as a good Greek writer does) subordinate clauses and participles. Bishop Lightfoot[4] had noted this long ago:

> There is an entire absence of periods for which the Greek language affords such facility. The sentences are co-ordinated not subordinated. The clauses are strung together, like beads on a string. The very monotony of arrange-

ment, though singularly impressive, is wholly unlike the Greek style of the age.

Parataxis is not necessarily Semitic—the 'and-and' style occurs also in vernacular Greek as well as in the speech of any English rustic raconteur. It is the excessive use of it which suggests Aramaic influence. Here are two out of many examples:

> He spat . . . and made . . . and put . . . and said (John 9.6f.).

> And all mine are thine, and thine are mine, and I am glorified in them. And I am no longer in the world, but they are in the world, and I am coming to thee. (John 17.10f.)

A third feature of John's style is what the grammarians call *asyndeton*, i.e. the lack of connecting particles. Anybody who has done Greek composition in school or college will remember how important it is to link up each sentence with the appropriate connective—a 'for' (*gar*), a 'therefore' (*oun*), a 'but' (*de*), and so on. Now asyndeton, or the absence of those connectives, is on the whole contrary to the genius of Greek, but it is highly characteristic of Aramaic. And 'asyndetic' John's Greek most certainly is. Not only does he write *legei* ('he says') and *legousin* ('they say') 'asyndetically' seventy times, but not one of the first twenty verses of John 15 has a connecting link-word. The over-use of asyndeton by John, especially when he is recording the sayings of Jesus, strongly suggests Aramaic influence.

Now let us note some of his grammatical constructions which point in the same direction.

Ten times—and all but once in direct speech—St John uses what seems a redundant pronoun. 1.27 is an example: 'of whom I am not worthy to untie the sandal-thong *of him* (*autou*).' This is a Semitism. Both Hebrew and Aramaic use a genderless and indeclinable relative which they follow up with a pronoun indicating case and gender.

Notice next, what the grammarians call 'a hanging case' (*casus pendens*). Here a sentence which starts with 'a hanging case' (generally nominative) is resumed and reinforced by an emphatic personal pronoun. St John produces this kind of sentence twenty-eight times. John 1.12 is a good instance: 'But *all who received him*, to them (Gk. *autois*) he gave etc.' This kind of construction is far commoner in Hebrew and Aramaic than in Greek, and it is the preponderance of it in John which suggests Aramaic influence.

Hebrew and Aramaic often use the indefinite third person plural instead of a passive tense. St John yields two examples, one on the lips of Jesus, 'They gather them and throw them in the fire' (John 15.6), the other on those of Mary Magdalene, 'They have taken away the Lord out of the tomb and we do not know where they have laid him' (John 20.2).

Finally, consider the quite remarkable over-use of *hina* ('in order that') in John's gospel. (He uses it one-hundred-and-twenty-nine times, twice or thrice as often as any of the other evangelists.) Now *hina* in *Koine* Greek had certainly grown much more versatile than it was in classical Greek where it normally expressed purpose. But John's unparalleled use of it suggests Aramaic influence. Burney held that John used it to translate—and sometimes to mistranslate—the indeclinable Aramaic d^e which was at once relative, conjunction and mark of the genitive. Many of Burney's alleged mistranslations can be explained without resort to an Aramaic hypothesis: even so, there remain some exceedingly odd uses of *hina* by John, as witness:

> 6.50: This is the bread which comes down from heaven *that* ('which') a man may eat of it and not die.
>
> 14.16: He will give you another Paraclete *that* ('who') he may be with you for ever. (Two old Latin MSS have *qui* here.)
>
> 16.2: The hour is coming *that* ('when') whoever kills you will think he is offering service to God.

In each case the oddity of John's Greek might reasonably be explained on the theory of an underlying Aramaic d^e. Once again it is the extraordinary over-use of *hina* by John which signals in an Aramaic direction.

But we can carry the argument for Aramaic influence one stage further. In his posthumous *The Poetry of our Lord* (1925) Burney showed that the sayings of Jesus in John often reveal that parallelism of Semitic poetry, found *passim* in the Psalms, which characterizes the words of Jesus in the synoptics (especially those drawn from 'Q' which almost certainly existed first in Aramaic). But he also showed that John's gospel has many sayings which, when translated into Aramaic, exhibit rhythm and rhyme. In 1946 Matthew Black[5] took Burney's work one stage further. Thus, if we put Jesus' saying in John 8.34 into Aramaic, we find clear evidence of word-play, since the Aramaic verb 'do' (*'abed*) and the Aramaic noun 'slave' (*'abd*) come from the same root: 'Everyone who does

sin is (its) slave.' So also in the Baptist's parable of the Bridegroom
and the Best Man (3.29f.), we find evidence of both strophic arrangement and assonance:

> He that hath the bride (*kall^etha*) is the bridegroom.
> He that standeth and heareth him is the friend of the bridegroom,
> And rejoiceth greatly because of the voice (*qala*) of the bridegroom.
> He must increase
> But I must decrease (*q^elal*)
> This my joy therefore is fulfilled (*k^elal*).

III

To sum up. The view that the fourth gospel is a straight translation
from an Aramaic original has not found support from either our
Semitists or our Hellenists. On the other hand, so stout an advocate
of Hellenistic influence in the fourth gospel as C. H. Dodd[6] can
write, 'The case for an underlying Semitic idiom is irresistible.'
John's is very much the kind of Greek which could have been written by a man whose mother-tongue was Aramaic.

According to Driver, Bultmann, T. W. Manson and M. Black, we
can go further. An Aramaic tradition—whether oral or written—
probably underlies the sayings of Jesus in the fourth gospel. It is
not unjustified to speak of some sort of Johannine 'Q'.

This point apart, only men like E. C. Colwell,[7] would demur to
the conclusion that, if St John wrote in Greek, he must have had
Aramaic as his mother-tongue. This is much the conclusion that
Lightfoot reached nearly one hundred years ago: 'It is not un-
grammatical Greek,' he wrote of John's style,[8] 'but it is distinctly
the Greek of one long accustomed to think and speak through the
medium of another language.'

NOTES

[1] *Life in Christ*, p. 29.

[2] Excellent survey in S. Brown's article 'From Burney to Black', *Catholic
Biblical Quarterly*, 26 (1964), pp. 323-339.

[3] *Biblical Essays* (1893), p. 135.

[4] Op. cit., p. 17.

[5] *An Aramaic Approach to the Gospels and Acts* (3rd edition, 1967),
pp. 171, 147.

[6] *I.F.G.*, p. 75.

[7] In *The Greek of the Fourth Gospel* (1931) Colwell declares that the
arguments of Burney and his followers do not justify the claim that John
thought or wrote in Aramaic.

[8] Op. cit., p. 16.

3

The Background of St John

THE fourth gospel's portrait of Jesus differs, *prima facie* at any rate, quite considerably from the synoptic one. In St John Jesus comes as a light into a dark world; he speaks with the accent of deity; he challenges men to decide for or against him as the incarnate truth of God. How did St John come to present him thus? Where are we to seek the background of his thought? In Hellenism? Or in Gnosticism? Or in Judaism?

Our main purpose in this chapter will be to draw out the affinities between John and the Dead Sea scrolls. But, in order to keep a proper balance, we must first review the many suggested sources for John's distinctive ways of thinking.

I

Although the gospel is in many ways redolent of Palestine, it was written in Greek and, according to tradition, in Ephesus, the city where, five centuries before, the Greek philosopher Heraclitus had spoken of a *Logos*. Some debt to Hellenism may, therefore, be presumed in John's book, and his use of *Logos* in his very first verse leads us to look for it. Accordingly, some have detected in John echoes of popular Platonism—compare his contrasts between that which is 'below' and that which is 'above' or between natural and 'real' bread with Plato's doctrine of Ideas. This need not surprise us, for popular Platonism was in the intellectual air of the time and had even infiltrated Judaism. (In addition to its horizontal, linear distinction between 'the present age' and 'the age to come', Jewish thought also drew a vertical distinction between the earthly and the heavenly.[1])

Again, many have suggested that John's thinking was influenced by Philo, the learned Jew of Alexandria (and a contemporary of Jesus) who combined Judaism and Hellenism, the claims of revelation and of reason, in order to make his faith intellectually respectable to Gentiles. Thus, to take one example only, if John talks of a *Logos* who is the mediator between God and men, so does Philo. But, though many good parallels have been found between them, the dependence of John on Philo is unproved. There is no 'hard' evidence that he was a student of Philo's works. Both owed much to the Old Testament, especially its Wisdom Literature. All we can safely posit is a common theological background and climate of thought.

Once again, others (notably Dodd) have sought light on John's background in the Hermetic writings which derive from Egypt and belong to the second and third centuries after Christ. These tractates take their name from a divine person Hermes Trismegistus (the Greek title of the Egyptian god Thoth), the first and best-known of them being *Poimandres*. Generally they blend Platonism and Stoicism with the religious thought of the Near East, in order to expound a mystical doctrine of salvation by knowledge. Many parallels of phrase and thought between John and the Hermetic books have been uncovered, e.g. 'light and life', 'abide in darkness', 'the water of immortality', etc. But the similarities should not be exaggerated, as the date of the Hermetic books obviously rules out any question of John's dependence on them.

II

From Hellenism we turn to Gnosticism. In the earlier decades of this century the History-of-Religions School (Reitzenstein, Bousset, etc.) found Gnostic influence in John. To define such a Protean thing as Gnosticism is difficult; but it included, besides a metaphysical dualism, belief in intermediate and hostile beings between God and man, the idea of the human soul as a divine spark imprisoned in matter, the need for knowledge gained through revelation if the soul was to win clear to light, the fewness of those capable of receiving salvation, the saving Revealer himself.

Gnosticism of this kind with the figure of Christ fitted into it, was once known to us only from the hostile comments of church fathers like Irenaeus and Hippolytus; but, thanks to the discovery in 1946 of a Gnostic library at Nag Hammadi in Egypt, we now have Gnostic gospels, like *The Gospel of Truth* and *The Gospel of Thomas*, to compare with John's.

That John, who wrote in the first century, was influenced by this kind of Hellenized Gnosticism which flowered rankly in the second, is quite unlikely. We have only to compare the new-found gospels with John to see how different they are. 'The findings at Nag Hammadi,' W. F. Albright[2] has said, 'show that these early Gnostics were even worse heretics than the Church Fathers supposed.'

On the other hand, the roots of this kind of thinking may well be older; and if Docetism—the tendency to deny the reality of Christ's humanity and suffering—be called Gnostic, we know that there is strong polemic against it in John's first epistle, and perhaps here and there in the gospel itself (e.g. John 19.34).

But was there conceivably a pre-Christian oriental brand of Gnosticism which influenced St John?

Between 1915 and 1925 the books of a Gnostic sect called the Mandeans—*Manda* means 'knowledge'—who take John the Baptist as their patron saint and survive to this day in Iraq, were made available to scholars through Lidzbarski's translations. A perusal of them showed that they contained words like 'life', 'light' and 'glory', symbols like water, bread and the shepherd, and the doctrine of a redeemer who had descended into the world of darkness to save his own before re-ascending into heaven. At once a 'Mandean fever' seized scholars like Bultmann. Though the Mandean books (an odd mixture of myth, fairy tale, theology, ethics and dubious history) date from the seventh or eighth century A.D., he argued that the sect was pre-Christian and provided John with many of his doctrines, including the myth of the redeemer. His argument, be it noted, was circular. He began by assuming there was Gnosticism in John and using John's gospel as his main source for reconstructing it. Then he invoked the late Mandean literature to confirm what he had found.

The 'Mandean fever' may now be said to have spent itself. By the judgment of his critics, Bultmann has not proved the pre-Christian origin of Mandaism. The probability is that the borrowing was the other way, and that the Mandeans are a late offshoot of Christianity.

III

We come now to the clearest source of all—the Old Testament and Palestinian Judaism.

St John has only a score of direct quotations from the Old Testament, but this is no measure of his debt to it. His first three words

'In the beginning' take us back to Genesis 1.1, as his ensuing doctrine of the *Logos* owes a great deal to the Old Testament concept of the Word of God. Go through the first six or seven chapters, and you will find Exodus echoes and motifs coming thick and fast —the paschal lamb, the prophet like Moses, the brazen serpent, the wilderness manna, the water from the rock. The 'I ams' of Messianic presence (e.g. John 8.24, 28) recall the 'I ams' of Yahweh in Isaiah (43.10, 25; 51.12). Deuteronomic echoes can be heard in the Farewell Discourses (cf. John 14.1 with Deut. 31.8 and John 14.15 with Deut. 7.9).

Again, the background for the 'shepherd' language of John 10 is Ezek. 34, as Psalm 80, in which God's people is likened to a vine God brought out of Egypt and even called 'the son of man', may well underlie Jesus' words about the true vine in John 15. The portrait of Jesus in John, as Raymond Brown[3] has clearly discerned, finds many parallels in what is said about the Divine Wisdom in books like Proverbs, Ecclesiasticus and the Wisdom of Solomon.

In short, the Old Testament is an essential and pervasive element in St John's background. So full is his mind with its riches— words, ideas, types—that they become quite naturally vehicles for expressing his understanding of the new faith.

The tradition of the Old Testament, preserved in writing, was also handed down in the ongoing life of Judaism, particularly rabbinical Judaism; and time and time again we come on something in John's gospel which can be illuminated by a knowledge of *rabbinica*.

Behind the reference to the Hidden Messiah (1.26; 7.27) we discern the rabbinical belief that the Messiah was waiting somewhere incognito—some said 'in the north', some 'in Rome'—till God should reveal him to Israel. When Jesus says to the Jews, 'you search the scriptures because you think that in them you have eternal life' (5.39), he was mocking the view of the rabbis that intensive study of the Torah was the way to eternal life. When the multitude invites Jesus to produce a sign like the manna in the fashion of Moses long before (6.31), we recall that according to the rabbis the renewal of the manna would be one of Messiah's gifts in the New Age. When Jesus says that the Jews permitted circumcision on the sabbath day (7.22f.), we remember the rabbis' ruling that the law about circumcision took precedence over the law about the sabbath: 'Great is circumcision,' said one of them, 'since it over-rides the stringent sabbath.'

Evidence like this once again underscores the Jewish affinities of John's gospel.

But rabbinical Judaism was not the only variety existent in the time of Christ. There was also sectarian Judaism. While Jesus was conducting his ministry in Galilee and Judea, there was living down on the shores of the Dead Sea a monastic community of Jews who, having quarrelled with the Jerusalem 'establishment', had settled in and around Qumran, there to pattern their lives on the precepts of the Torah (as they interpreted it) and to await the Day of the Lord. These men are now generally identified with the Essenes whom we know of from Josephus and Pliny; their sacred books are the Dead Sea scrolls; and they shed light on the New Testament as a whole, but especially on the background of John's gospel.

To them, for the rest of this chapter, we must now turn.

IV

'In these new texts,' wrote K. G. Kuhn[4] in 1950, 'we are for the first time in contact with the native soil of John's gospel.' A tall claim indeed when we remember the many attempts made in the last half-century to fix the affinities of John's thought-world! Did Kuhn over-state his case? Against him and other champions of the scrolls many have preferred the charge of 'Scrollomania'. And no doubt the number of parallels and contacts between John's gospel and the Dead Sea scrolls has been considerably exaggerated by some in their initial enthusiasm; but what makes their discovery important is that, for the first time, they give us a body of thought which may provide an actual background for the fourth gospel, both in date and place (southern Palestine in the first century B.C./A.D.) and in basic theological affinity.

To put it another way, a document like the *Manual of Discipline* (the 'rules book' of the community) shows that down at Qumran, only an hour from the Judean scenes of our Lord's ministry, lived Jews who used the distinctive theological categories and idioms which we have been wont to call 'Johannine' and which, till recently, have often been dated to the second century and labelled 'Gnostic' and Greek.

Anyone who studies the *Manual* will not have gone far before he lights on the phrase 'do the truth' which is at once quite un-Greek and quite Johannine (cf. John 3.21 'He who does the truth comes to the light'; cf. I John 1.6). A few lines more, and he will find a reference to 'the sons of light'—a phrase used by Christ in John 12.36. A little later, an allusion to him who 'looks at the light of life' will recall Christ's promise of 'the light of life' to the man who follows him (John 8.10).

> By his (God's) knowledge everything has been brought into being
> And everything that is, he established by his purpose,
> And apart from him nothing is done

will ring a Johannine bell in his memory—

> All things were made through him,
> And without him was not anything made that was made (John 1.2).

In a passage about the two spirits—'the spirit of truth and the spirit of error' (cf. I John 4.6)—which dominate men's lives, he will learn that 'the sons of error walk in the ways of darkness' and remember Christ's warning against 'walking in darkness' (John 12.35). Finally, here is a Qumran contrast between the wise man and the foolish—

> According to each man's inheritance in truth he does right, and so he hates error; but according to his possession in the lot of error he does wickedly in it, and so he abhors the truth

which is reminiscent of John 3.20f.—

> For everyone who does evil hates the light, and does not come to the light, lest his deeds should be exposed. But he who does what is true comes to the light that it may be clearly seen that his deeds have been wrought in God.

But the links between the scrolls and John are more than linguistic and literary.

(i) Consider first St John's account of the Baptist, which differs considerably from the synoptic one. Do the scrolls help in any way to confirm it?

'Bethany beyond Jordan' (1.28) where the Baptist worked cannot, as the crow flies, have been far from Qumran. That the Baptist had a direct association with Qumran has not been proved, yet it is altogether likely that he knew something of the beliefs and practices of the sectarians there. Not only so, they held one or two theological points in common.[5]

According to John 1.19-23 the Baptist, denying that he was either the Messiah, or Elijah, or the prophet like Moses (an important

figure in the Qumran theology as in John's) told the enquiring depu-
tation from Jerusalem, 'I am the voice of one crying in the wilderness, "Make straight the way of the Lord", as the prophet Isaiah
said.' Now the scrolls show that the saints of Qumran used precisely the same text, Isa. 40.3, to describe their role in the divine
plan. This is how their marching orders ran:

> They will separate themselves from the midst of the habitation of per-
> verse men to go to the wilderness to clear there the way of the Lord,
> as it is written:
> 'In the wilderness clear the way of the Lord;
> Level in the desert a highway for our God' (I QS viii, 13f.).

They believed they would prepare the way by a more rigorous
concentration on the Law of Moses, which is hardly what the
Baptist had in mind. But if they used Isa. 40.3 to describe their
raison d'être, we need not doubt that the Baptist did the same, as
John says he did.

According to John 1.26f., 33, the Baptist, asserting that his
baptism was a preliminary one of water, predicted that the
Mightier One would baptize with the Holy Spirit. With this we
may compare the passage in the *Manual* (I QS iv, 20-3) which declares that in the Messianic age

> God will purge by his truth all the deeds of men, refining for himself
> some of mankind, in order to abolish every evil spirit from the midst of
> his flesh, and to cleanse him through a Holy Spirit from all wicked
> practices, sprinkling upon him a Spirit of truth as purifying water.

Here, in a context of judgment, we find the men of Qumran
predicting that their own purifyings in water would, in the
Messianic age, be superseded by a divine cleansing with the Holy
Spirit.[6]

(ii) Now let us turn to something basic to the scrolls and St
John. Every student of the fourth gospel and John's epistles must
have remarked the great antitheses—light and darkness, truth and
error, spirit and flesh, life and death—which sound a kind of
counterpoint through John's thinking and writing. This is the
language of dualism; and not so long ago it was fashionable among
scholars to find in it clear evidence that John's thought was
moulded by the dualistic categories—Greek and metaphysical—
which are to be found in the second-century Gnostics. The discovery of the scrolls has made them think again, for the closest

parallels to John's antitheses are now generally acknowledged to occur not among the second-century Gnostics but in the Qumran documents written just before the time of Christ.

This brings us to the cardinal point on which most of our scholars (Kuhn, Albright, Burrows, Cross, Allegro, Brownlee, Reicke, Jeremias and Brown) speak with almost one voice: the dualism which pervades the Johannine writings is of precisely the same sort as we find in the scrolls: not physical or substantial (as in the Gnostics) but monotheistic, ethical and eschatological.

To say that the dualism is monotheistic is another way of saying that it is a modified—not a thorough-going dualism. The opposition between light and darkness is not between two eternal and equipollent powers but between two created powers both of which exist under the sovereignty of God. (Here the influence of Old Testament monotheism is plain.)

Next, the dualism is ethical. Just as for St John 'light' is primarily the symbol of sheer goodness, as 'darkness' is of moral evil, so it is for the men of Qumran.

Finally the dualism is (as in Iranian thought whence it may have come) eschatological. Both the authors of the scrolls and St John see history as the scene of a great battlefield in which light struggles for the mastery with darkness. But if the Qumran saints see the End lying in the near future—on the far side of some Armageddon, as in the *War Scroll*—St John declares that the End has already begun.

What shall we conclude? 'No longer,' answers Allegro,[7] 'can John be regarded as the most Hellenistic of the evangelists; his "gnosticism" and the whole framework of his thought is seen now to spring directly from a Jewish sectarianism rooted in Palestinian soil.'

Having made our main point about this shared dualism, we may now usefully point out some contrasts between John and Qumran.

First: both St John and the men of Qumran believe, as we should expect of people who share the heritage of the Old Testament, in the creation of everything by God. Again, both see the world of men as ranged in two opposing camps of light and darkness, each with a personal leader. But, whereas for the men of Qumran the leader of the sons of light is an angel, i.e. a created being, for St John he is the eternal Word of God made flesh.

Second: both believe that 'there is a war on'. But whereas for the Qumran saints it is a ding-dong struggle not to be decided till the last great battle between the sons of light and the sons of darkness, for St John the victory is, in large measure, already won —by his victory in the Cross and Resurrection Christ has triumphed over the ruler of darkness and his minions, so that it may be claimed that 'the true light is already shining' (I John 2.8). Here, incidentally, we may note that when we read in John's Prologue 'the true light was coming into the world', he is thinking not of the light of reason—the inner light—but of the light of the new creation—the eschatological light.

Third: both St John and the scrolls agree that the answer to the question, What must I do to be saved? is, You must become a son of light. But whereas the Qumran view is that this means obedience to the Law of Moses as interpreted in Qumran—and this implies a legalism which outgoes even 'the tradition of the elders' in the gospels—for St John it means the acceptance by faith of Christ as the one true light of the world.

In a word, the basic difference between the scrolls and the fourth gospel is, as we might have expected, the Fact of Christ.

(iii) There are other ways in which John and the men of the scrolls may be shown to speak common theological language. For instance, both the fourth gospel and the scrolls set strong stress on unity and community. Indeed, the Essenes' name for themselves as the Community is literally the Unity (*hyhd* : 'togetherness'), and for them this one-ness is a sign that the New Age is at hand. When, therefore, we find in John phrases like 'gather into one' (11.52), 'that they may be one' (17.11) and 'that they may become perfectly one' (17.23), we might almost suppose that he was talking the language of Qumran.[8]

But, to round off our discussion, let us consider what the sectarians and St John have to say about 'truth', which is a key-word for them both. In his gospel John uses the word (*alētheia*) twenty-five times; and 'truth' (*'mt*) figures very prominently in the vocabulary of Qumran. We have already noted that both St John and the sectarians speak of 'doing the truth' and 'walking in the truth'. The Jewish ring of both phrases is unmistakable: truth is something to be practised or done—it has an existential flavour about it. In the same way the scrolls speak of 'witnessing to truth', as St John does (John 5.33; 18.37). Similarly, when the scrolls say that 'God will purify all the deeds of men by his truth', we remember how Christ prayed that his disciples would be 'sanctified by the truth' (John 17.17).

But perhaps the most interesting 'truth' parallel concerns St John's doctrine of the Spirit.

In the Farewell Discourses, the Holy Spirit, who is to be 'the presence of Jesus when he is absent', is named the Paraclete or Advocate, and characterized as 'the Spirit of truth'. His role is not only to indwell the disciples, teaching and guiding them 'into all the truth', but to bear witness for Christ and to prove the world wrong, i.e. he is to have a *juridical* as well as a didactic function. Can we shed any light on the origin of this juridical aspect of the Spirit's work?

Thirty years ago S. Mowinckel[9] traced this concept of the Spirit back to the *Testaments of the Twelve Patriarchs* (a Pharisaic work written about 100 B.C.) which may well have had Essene connexions. In the Testament of Judah, chapter 20 we have not only a reference to 'the spirit of truth and the spirit of error' (as in I John 4.6), but the statement that 'the Spirit of truth *bears witness* and *accuses* of everything' so that 'the sinner is on fire in his heart and cannot lift his face to his judge'.

If we turn now to the *Manual* and the *War Scroll* from Qumran we find 'the Spirit of truth', or 'the Prince of light', depicted as the helper or vindicator of the sons of light. This Spirit not only testifies to the truth in the hearts of those in the 'inheritance' of truth, but accuses the children of darkness.[10] His role, in fact, is that of St John's Advocate Spirit of truth who 'will convict the world of sin and of righteousness and of judgment' (John 16.8). In the light of this evidence we may claim that we now understand John's doctrine and its Jewish antecedents with some clarity. It is a doctrine which has some relevance for us today. The Paraclete exercises his ministry through Christians and the way of life to which they bear witness. The only way today 'the world' can know that Jesus' death was not the end, is that the Spirit which indwelt Jesus is still at work in his followers.

> This is how the Paraclete proves the world wrong and shows that Jesus is triumphant with the Father, while the Prince of this world has been condemned, namely, that, two thousand years after Jesus' death his presence is still made visible in his disciples; through Christians the Paraclete is still glorifying Jesus.[11]

Enough has been said to show how the scrolls illuminate the

background of John's gospel. We must, however, be careful not to overstate our case by suggesting that Qumran parallels can be found for most things in St John. In the decisive matters concerning the person of Christ we get little or no help from the scrolls. Moreover, when a modern scholar[12] declares that 'the Scrolls have helped to indicate that John need never have set foot outside of Palestine nor heard of Plato, Philo or the Stoics in order to have held the world view that he did', we may feel that he has overstressed the Jewishness of the gospel. Finally, as Jeremias[13] reminds us, we must also remember that the theologies of both the New Testament and of the scrolls have a common root in the Old Testament. But what we may agree about is that

> the Fourth Gospel is not to be interpreted against the background of Gnostic presuppositions but against that of Palestinian Old Testament theological thinking, and of a piety rooted and grounded in the Bible.

Note: Jesus as the Wisdom of God

When St John undertook to set forth the *Mysterium Christi*, he chose (as Paul also did) the highest interpretative category known to Judaism, that of the personified Wisdom of God found in the Old Testament sapiential books like Proverbs, Ecclesiasticus and the Wisdom of Solomon.

According to them (Prov. 8.22f.; Ecclus. 24.9; Wisd. 9.9) Wisdom pre-existed with God. So did Jesus (John 1.1; 17.5).

Dwelling in heaven, Wisdom descended to earth and tabernacled in Israel (Bar. 3.37; Prov. 8.31; Ecclus. 24.8). So did Jesus (John 1.14; 3.31; 6.38, 16.28).

Wisdom was an emanation of God's glory (Wisd. 7.25). Jesus was the divine glory incarnate and manifested it to men (John 1.14; 8.50; 11.4; 17.5).

Wisdom teaches men heavenly things (Wisd. 9.16), tells them what pleases God (Wisd. 8.4) and thus leads them to life (Prov. 8.35; Ecclus. 4.12). So does Jesus (John 3.19; 5.40; 14.19). Just as Wisdom discourses in the first person to her hearers, (Prov. 8; Ecclus. 24), so Jesus addresses men, often beginning with 'I am'. Using the symbols of food and drink (Prov. 9.2-5; Ecclus. 24.19-21), Wisdom invites men to eat and drink. These same symbols Jesus employs of his revelation (John 4.13f.; 6.35, 51ff.).

Again, if Wisdom 'seeks' men (Prov. 8.1ff.; Wisd. 6.16) and cries aloud her invitation in public places, Jesus seeks men out (John 5.14; 9.35) and publicly cries out his invitation (John 7.28, 37; 12.44). As Wisdom instructs disciples (Wisd. 6.17-19) who are her children (Prov. 8.32f.; Ecclus. 6.18), Jesus gathers disciples whom he names 'little children' (13.33). And, as Wisdom 'tests' her disciples (Ecclus. 6.20-26) till they love her (Prov. 8.17; Ecclus. 4.12; Wisd. 6.17f.) and become 'friends of God' (Wisd. 7.14, 27), so Jesus 'tests' his disciples (6.67) till he can call them his 'friends' (John 15.15) and cleanse and sanctify them by his word and truth (John 15.2; 17.17).

Thus both in the Prologue and in the body of his gospel St John has pressed Wisdom motifs into the service of his Christology. Had he, so to say, Dominical warrant for doing this? Already in the synoptics we find Jesus speaking *in persona Sapientiae*:

> Yet Wisdom is justified by all her children (Luke 7.35).
>
> The wisdom of Solomon . . . something greater than Solomon is here (Luke 11.31).
>
> Therefore also the Wisdom of God said . . . (Luke 11.49).
>
> Come unto me, all ye that labour, etc. (Matt. 11.28-30),

(where Jesus echoes the appeal of Wisdom in Ecclus. 51.23-27). It looks as if St John were developing something present in the early gospel tradition, something which goes back to Jesus himself.

On the whole subject see R. Brown's pages in his Anchor Bible Commentary, cxxii-xxv. He rightly claims that we have here better parallels to John's thought than any produced from the Hermetic and Mandean books.

NOTES

[1] R. E. Brown, *A.B.S.J.*, CXV.

[2] *The Background of the New Testament and its Eschatology*, p. 162.

[3] See note at the end of this chapter.

[4] Z. *Th.K.*, xlvii, 1950, p. 210.

[5] John's baptism and the lustrations of the Essenes seem to have resembled each other in various respects: each was combined with a strong demand for prior repentance; each was for those who were Jews already (not for pagans desiring to embrace Judaism); and each was designed to create a penitent nucleus in Israel before the coming of the Day of the Lord.

[6] On the whole subject see W. H. Brownlee's 'John the Baptist in the New Light of the Ancient Scrolls' in *The Scrolls and the New Testament*.

[7] *The Dead Sea Scrolls*, p. 128.

[8] F. M. Cross, *The Ancient Library of Qumran*, p. 155f.

[9] Z.N.W., 32 (1933), pp. 97-130.

[10] See F. M. Cross in *The Interpreter's Bible*, XII, pp. 661f.

[11] Vide R. Brown's article in *N.T. S.* Jan. 1967, pp. 113-132. *Inter alia*, he shows how improbable is Bultmann's view that St John's Paraclete is an adaptation of the Mandean *Jawar* or Revealer.

[12] F. H. Borsch, *The Son of Man in Myth and History*, p. 257.

[13] E.T. Dec. 1958, p. 69.

4

The Gospel Tradition of St John

I

D I D St John know and use the synoptic gospels, or did he have access to independent and early tradition? In the last fifty years this question has sharply divided the critics. In 1924—as witness the 14th chapter of Streeter's *The Four Gospels*—the critics were generally agreed that John knew Mark and probably Luke. This consent rested on two considerations: (1) John's gospel has the same general outline as Mark's; and (2) when John tells a story about Jesus, like the Anointing at Bethany, he seems to betray his dependence on him by repeating some of Mark's phrases, e.g. 'ointment of pure nard'. More than anything else this apparent dependence of John on Mark—and possibly Luke—helped to discredit him as an original witness and to make any connexion of the gospel with the son of Zebedee look highly improbable; for how could John represent a first-hand tradition about Jesus if in fact he needed to rely on Mark and Luke, neither of them among the Twelve?

Today this view is widely abandoned for two reasons: (1) the rediscovery of the apostolic *kerygma*, and (2) a fresh realization of the part played by oral tradition in the early Church.

'In the beginning was the *kerygma*', a proclamation of God's saving action in Christ whose outline we may recover by a comparison of certain 'traditional' passages in Paul (e.g. I Cor. 15.3ff.) with the apostolic speeches in 'early' Acts (e.g. Acts 10.36-43). If then John's gospel reveals the same general outline of the Story of Jesus as Mark's, this is because they both independently reflect the shape of the *kerygma* which was common to all the traditions within the Church: there is no question of John having borrowed from Mark.

Before the rise, in the 'twenties', of the Form Critics, theories of literary dependence were the order of the day. Similarities in outline and in detail between John and Mark were therefore plausibly explained by the assumption that John did in fact know Mark. But when Form Criticism had done its work on the pre-literary tradition underlying the gospels, not only did the part played by oral tradition gain a new importance, but scholars realized anew that it continued to be a vital factor right through New Testament times. Even at the beginning of the second century Papias preferred 'the living voice'. So, whereas Streeter and his compeers took slight verbal resemblances between John and Mark as proof of John's dependence on Mark, nowadays critics discount small similarities as things easily remembered and likely to become stereotyped in oral tradition, and rightly demand a high percentage of verbal agreement plus agreement in order before they will concede the case for literary dependence.

With these prolegomena, we may now briefly survey a debate which began in 1938 with Gardner-Smith's slim but seminal *St John and the Synoptic Gospels* and may be said to have reached a decisive climax with C. H. Dodd's *Historical Tradition in the Fourth Gospel* (1963).

II

Gardner-Smith did three things: (1) He challenged the view of critical orthodoxy that the fourth gospel showed clear dependence on one or more of the synoptics. The number of texts where dependence can be plausibly argued (he said) is very small, and even in them the disagreements outnumber the agreements. Moreover, the total plan of John diverges so greatly from that of the synoptics that it must be independent.

(2) He argued cogently that the resemblances spring from the fact that all the evangelists drew upon a common store of oral tradition.

(3) He concluded by suggesting that we could no longer simply assume that John's was the fourth gospel, and that, if the argument of his book was sound, John was an independent authority for the Story of Jesus. Should this view gain ground, a new chapter (he declared) would have opened in the criticism of the gospels and the study of Christian origins.

With the outbreak of the Second World War scholarly reactions were inevitably slow to appear. The first significant one came in 1943 from an acknowledged expert on the fourth gospel. 'I am

almost persuaded,' said W. F. Howard,[1] 'by the cumulative force
of Gardner-Smith's argument.' In 1951 Rudolf Bultmann[2] asserted
that John's knowledge of the synoptics had not been proved. Two
years later C. H. Dodd[3] (who had previously agreed with Streeter)
was writing: 'How fragile are the arguments by which the dependence of John on the other gospels has been "proved"!' In 1956
T. W. Manson[4] observed:

> There is a growing body of opinion that the Fourth Gospel enshrines a
> tradition of the Ministry which is independent of the Synoptic accounts,
> bears distinct marks of its Palestinian origin, and is on some points
> possibly superior to the Synoptic record. The question of the historical
> view of the Fourth Gospel is wide open again.

To be sure, not all the pundits were persuaded. When C. K.
Barrett's learned documentary on John appeared in 1955, he was
found to be firmly behind Streeter, as was R. H. Lightfoot whose
posthumous commentary on the gospel came out a year later.

These were mostly British pronouncements. Meantime, however,
notable support for Gardner-Smith came from Denmark. In his
Zur Johanneischen Tradition (1954) Bent Noack championed the
case for oral tradition against all theories of literary dependence.
After a detailed rebuttal of Bultmann (who in his commentary had
argued that John, though independent of the synoptics, used two
main literary sources, one for the 'Signs', the other for the Johannine discourses) Noack went on to study the *logia* peculiar to John,
his Old Testament quotations, his synoptic-like *pericopae*, and his
narratives. Similarities between, say, John 12.1-8 and Mark 14.3-9
(the Anointing) he explained (a) by the view that identical verbal
sequences are just the kind of thing likely to have been preserved
identically even in oral tradition and (b) by later scribal assimila-
tion of John's text to the synoptics. The quotations from the Old
Testament were probably made from memory. In fact, John's
links with the synoptics were quite inadequate to establish a
literary relationship between them, and the features of John's
narrative style suggested not dependence on the synoptics but
derivation from oral tradition. John's fondness for '*Hoti* recitative'
followed by direct speech, his repetition of key-phrases, his allusions to 'writing' (20.30f.; 21.24f.), all implied that John was writing down for the first time what, till then, had existed in the oral
tradition of some Church uninfluenced by the synoptic tradition.

His conclusion was that John used no written source: all was derived from the memory or knowledge of the writer.

If the Danish scholar had not answered all the questions, he had certainly made Gardner-Smith's thesis look much more probable.

Through the 'fifties and into the 'sixties the debate continued, its to's and fro's reflected in many of the articles appearing in *New Testament Studies*. Thus Peder Borgen[5] thought that John followed an independent tradition but that at certain points in the Passion Story we find fused units from the oral tradition behind the synoptics. E. D. Johnston[6] picked out five non-Marcan features in John's story of the Feeding of the Five Thousand which had a good claim to be accounted historical, and so made a case for John's independence in this narrative. The American P. Parker[7] discussing the links between John and the synoptics, especially Luke, found that John did not know the synoptics. His links with them came from a common oral tradition; and it was possible that John and Luke worked in the same areas for a time and heard the same traditions about Jesus.

Another example of the new trend was A. J. B. Higgins's *The Historicity of the Fourth Gospel* (1960). Here again John's independence is maintained. To be sure, John used some traditions similar to those in the synoptics, but he drew also on others, some perhaps going back to the Apostle John—and he interwove all with his own interpretative material. Two Johannine narratives, which occur also in the synoptics, are carefully examined. The healing of the Officer's Son is shown to have come from a tradition parallel to the synoptic story of the Centurion's Servant (or Boy) and to be, historically, not inferior to it. After a comparison of the events in John 6 (the Feeding, the Walking on the water, the Defection, the Confession) with Mark 6-8, he judges that John's account hangs together better than Mark's. If these two narratives come so well out of the comparison, the presumption is that other narratives in John may well come from good tradition. John's accounts of the concurrent ministries of the Baptist and of Jesus, of Jesus' several visits to Jerusalem, of his withdrawal 'beyond Jordan', of the informal enquiry before Annas plus the personal names found in John's gospel, have all a claim to historicity. Finally, he argues that the Johannine *logia* often rest back on traditional sayings of Jesus, that his Old Testament quotations reflect primitive Christian *testimonia*, and that his place-names are not invented. The conclusion is that the sources or traditions used by St John deserve as much respect as those employed in the synoptics.

Higgins had paved the way for C. H. Dodd's *Historical Tradition in the Fourth Gospel* (1963). So important is it that it deserves a section to itself.

III

In his earlier book on the interpretation of the gospel, Dodd had suggested that John had access to early traditions and was not writing a symphony on synoptic themes. In *Historical Tradition* he works out these hints in impressive detail, wedding a wise Form Criticism to great learning in order to show that in no case need we postulate John's dependence on the synoptics, and that he is a witness to the early traditions of the Church worthy to stand alongside the synoptics.

In Part I of his book he begins with the Passion Story which, as scholars now agree, was the first part of the Gospel tradition to attain the form of a continuous narrative. John's account conforms to the traditional pattern, but its amount of verbal resemblance to the synoptics is almost the minimum possible if the same story is to be told at all. Rather the nature of his narrative suggests an independent rendering of oral tradition parallel with Mark's and with the non-Marcan tradition which forms the basis of Luke's Passion Story. A study of his Old Testament quotations, or *testimonia*, shows an understanding of the Passion which is pre-canonical and primitive. (Here Dodd takes the same line as in his earlier *According to the Scriptures*.) If we study one by one the various episodes in John's Passion narrative, we will find nothing to compel belief that he conflated materials from the synoptics and much to make us believe he was drawing on independent sources. Moreover, the contacts of John's narrative with Jewish tradition and the political situation (the tension between Rome and Judea) suggest that his account of Jesus' Trial goes back to the years before the final extinction of Jewish autonomy, i.e. is pre-A.D. 66.

A study of John's account of the 'Prelude to the Passion' (the Entry, the Cleansing, the Anointing) again indicates his independence. The healing miracles of the fourth gospel are cast in the same mould as similar stories in the synoptics, but are independently derived from oral tradition. John's narrative of the Feeding and its sequel comes from a tradition superior to that underlying the synoptic record, and preserves knowledge of the unstable political situation in which Jesus was in peril of becoming involved. It is improbable that the difficult stories of the miracle at Cana and the raising of Lazarus were inspired by anything in the synoptic tradition. Lastly, the 'travel traditions' in the gospel and the Palestinian place-names, so far from being the evangelist's invention, reflect pre-Johannine tradition owing nothing to the synoptics.

In the fourth gospel's account of John the Baptist and the call of the first disciples Dodd once again finds clear evidence of independent tradition, and he draws attention to the remarkable coincidence between the Johannine and the rabbinic traditions that Jesus had originally *five* disciples.

Part II discusses the sayings of Jesus in the fourth gospel. First, Dodd uncovers five 'dialogues' in John similar to those in the synoptics but obviously independent. Next, he draws a like conclusion concerning sixteen 'Words of the Lord' common to the synoptics and the fourth gospel. Special interest attaches to his discovery of half a dozen miniature parables which, though peculiar to John, have a good right to be accounted authentic. Then, after laying bare some sequences of traditional sayings (e.g. those about the harvest in John 4.35ff.), he ends his study by arguing that the predictive teaching of Jesus found in the Farewell Discourses, originally ambiguous in expression, more faithfully reflects the mind of Jesus than the more apocalyptic version preserved in the synoptics.

Dodd rightly says that the argument of his book is 'cumulative and interlocking'. Indeed it is, for it builds up, point by point, to its conclusion, that behind the fourth gospel lies an ancient oral tradition, independent of the synoptics. Existing originally in Aramaic, it has a clear Jewish setting and reflects the political situation in southern Palestine before the outbreak of the war between Judea and Rome. From this tradition derive not only John's Passion Story but the various *pericopae*, 'Words of the Lord', parables, miracle-stories, travel-traditions and place-names we have mentioned. This tradition we may use to supplement or correct the synoptic one, and so construct a better account of the works and words of the Jesus of history.

But if Dodd's argument is cumulative and interlocking, it is also compelling and convincing. Those who will take the trouble to re-

read Streeter's chapter and compare it with Dodd's treatment of the whole subject will not only realize how much New Testament science has progressed since 1925, but will be compelled to admit that the weight of evidence is clearly on Dodd's side. In his book the long debate we have been sketching reaches a decisive climax; henceforward all who would follow Streeter must demolish the massive argumentation of *Historical Tradition*. For ourselves, we have no doubt that Dodd has proved his case. This too is the judgment of Raymond E. Brown, the distinguished American Roman Catholic scholar, in his recent massive commentary on the fourth gospel.

> John [he writes] drew on an independent source of tradition about Jesus, similar to the sources that underlie the Synoptics . . . John is based on a solid tradition of the works and words of Jesus, a tradition which is at times very primitive. We believe that often John gives us correct historical information about Jesus that no other Gospel has preserved.[8]

IV

If then we are agreed that the work of Dodd and his predecessors has immensely strengthened the case for taking the fourth gospel seriously as a quarry for historical facts, let us briefly itemize and evaluate the 'traditional' elements in John.

(a) *Travels and Topography*

When we study transitional passages in the gospel like 3.22f.

> After this Jesus and his disciples went into the land of Judea; there he remained with them and baptized. John also was baptizing at Aenon near Salim, because there was much water there; and people came and were baptized,

the use of imperfect tenses and the presence of topographical data strongly suggest that John is not freely composing tiny 'travelogues' for Jesus but reproducing traditional information about his journeys. Other examples are 2.12; 4.1-3; 4.43f.; 10.40ff.; and 11.54.

So too with the place-names of the fourth gospel (to be discussed in a later chapter). St John is not inventing them as he goes along: he is working on information which he had received and considered trustworthy; and modern archaeological research, as we shall see, often confirms its accuracy. Moreover, if John mentions many places in Judea, Samaria and Transjordan (Sychar, Aenon, Bethesda, Gabbatha, etc.) not found in the synoptics, this 'southern' slant to his topography was never 'dreamed up' in Ephesus, but points to a pre-Johannine tradition with a special interest in southern Palestine and Transjordan.

(b) *John the Baptist*

The fourth evangelist's primary interest in the Baptist is as a witness to Christ, and he has little to say about the prophet of impending judgment depicted for us by the synoptists. But it would be wrong to conclude that in our 'quest for the historical John' we must rely only on the synoptics and Josephus. Analysis reveals in the fourth gospel, especially in 1.19-37 (John's testimony at Bethany beyond Jordan) and 3.22-30 (John at Aenon near Salim) pre-Johannine tradition about the Baptist. This reflects current Jewish beliefs and language—the use of Isa. 40.3, Elijah as Messiah's forerunner, the doctrine of the hidden Messiah, the title 'Lamb of God', etc.— which have all the marks of historical trustworthiness.

(c) *The First Disciples and the Early Ministry*

In St John's account of the first disciples, e.g. the naming of Peter and the call of Philip (1.42-44), and more clearly in his record of the Baptist's activity at Aenon (3.22-30), there survive traces of independent tradition at the disposal of the evangelist. We learn that two of Jesus' first adherents had once belonged to the Baptist's circle and that Jesus may originally have had a group of *five* disciples (as the Talmud says); that Jesus exercised an early ministry in Judea concurrent with the Baptist's at Aenon (something almost implied by Matt. 11.16-19; Luke 7.31-35) and including like his, the rite of baptism (3.22 'Jesus . . . baptized'—'an undigested scrap of genuine information'.[9] (Cf. 4.2); and that his work in the south ended—perhaps owing to the hostility of the Pharisees—with his departure to Galilee. Most of these statements commend themselves as historically credible, and later in this book we shall have something to say about the pre-Galilean ministry of Jesus.

(d) *The Galilean Ministry*

The Galilean ministry receives much greater attention from the synoptics than it does from John. Nonetheless, in the record of that Ministry's decisive climax—the Feeding of the Five Thousand and what followed it—only the independent tradition underlying John

6 makes proper sense of the events recorded in Mark 6.30-8.33. (John 6.66-71 is obviously the Johannine equivalent of Peter's Confession at Caesarea Philippi, narrated in Mark 8.27-33.) Here St John can be shown to have knowledge of a tradition which closely connected Peter's Confession with the Feeding and its sequel—a connexion obscured by Mark's duplicate version of the Feeding (8.1-10) and by the intrusion of other material.

John illuminates details in Mark's story of the Feeding (five thousand *men*, in companies of hundreds and fifties—a quasi-military formation). He supplies answers to questions left unanswered by Mark (e.g. why did Jesus *compel* his disciples to depart in a boat across the Lake and then stay behind to disperse the crowd before retiring alone to the hills?). He records the later defection of many followers (6.66) and so enables us to appreciate the crisis caused by the Feeding.

What emerges from a critical comparison of John 6 with Mark 6-8 is a flood of new light on the potentially dangerous *political* situation in which Jesus was in danger of becoming embroiled. Thus,

> when the people saw the sign which had been done, they said, 'This is indeed the prophet who is to come into the world!' Perceiving then that they were about to come and take him by force to make him king, Jesus withdrew again to the hills by himself (John 6.14f.).

As a direct result of the Feeding a Messianic 'revolt in the desert' was brewing. (This consists well with all that Josephus has to tell about false prophets and Messianic pretenders in those days.) Now we begin to understand why Jesus acted as Mark says he did. Aware of the attempt to force his mission into a political channel, he deliberately resisted it by separating his close followers from the rest and going himself into seclusion. The result was to disappoint many of his adherents and cause widespread disaffection, so that eventually the Twelve remained as a faithful remnant with whom a fresh start could be made.

'Will you also go away?' These poignant words supply a plausible reason for the question of Jesus recorded by Mark, 'But you—who do you say that I am?' which evoked the confession of Peter. That confession was the direct result of the disaffection among Jesus' followers recorded only by St John. The whole sequence of events not only hangs together but preserves a convincing explanation of what must have been a turning-point in the ministry.

(e) *The Sayings of Jesus*

How far does St John add to our knowledge of what the Jesus of history actually said?

Quite certainly the evangelist had at his disposal many traditional sayings of Jesus. The trouble is that, since he has a way of passing all he takes over through the crucible of his own mind and putting his stamp upon it, it is often hard to determine what is traditional *logion* and what Johannine interpretation. Later we shall see that many utterances of Jesus in the fourth gospel may be described as 'inspired airs based on original themes'. In the meanwhile let us briefly set down some obviously traditional elements in the Johannine account of Jesus' words.

First, we must mention the half dozen *dialogues* between Jesus and his disciples, or his critics, which must rest back on real tradition, e.g. Jesus and his disciples on food (4.31-34), Peter's confession (6.67-70), Jesus and his brothers (7.3ff.), and Jesus and the blind man at Siloam (9.2-5).

Next, we have about a dozen short *parables* (to be discussed later).

To these add some two dozen '*synoptic-like sayings*', i.e. sayings which, because they resemble synoptic logia, have a claim to rank as 'Words of the Lord'. We may add that there must be many more in the gospel, not now identifiable because we cannot parallel them from the synoptics.[10]

Finally, to these we may add the *predictive sayings* of Jesus contained in the Farewell Discourses. These, in the opinion of scholars like C. H. Dodd, J. A. T. Robinson, and E. Stauffer, more accurately reflect our Lord's mind about the future than the more apocalyptic *logia* of the synoptic gospels.

(f) *The Healing Miracles of Jesus*

Because he was selecting among 'many signs' (John 20.30), St John's gospel does not contain the wealth of healing miracles found in the synoptics. But three of those he does relate—the Officer's Son (another version of the Centurion's Boy), the Cripple at Bethesda and the Man born Blind—move entirely within the ambience of the traditional healing miracles in the synoptics and have as good a claim to historicity as they. One feature of them, which has all the marks of truth upon it, is our Lord's demand for the patient's co-operation in the cure: 'Have you the will to health?' he says to the Bethesda Cripple; 'Go and wash in the Pool of Siloam,' he commands the Man born Blind.

The story of the raising of Lazarus, as is well known, presents special difficulties. As it lies before us now, it has been 'written up' by the evangelist; but in view of the circumstantial details it contains and the abundant evidence that St John had access to good independent tradition, the one thing we ought not to do is to dismiss it as John's creation out of nothing—or as a miraculous quilt made out of synoptic patches.

It is perhaps worth noting that three of these healing miracles were wrought in Jerusalem or near it—which is evidence that our Lord's healing ministry was not confined to Galilee.

(g) *The Passion Story*

Scholars have long argued—and Dodd's brilliant discussion greatly strengthens their case—that John's whole story of the Passion, from his leave-taking of the disciples to the appearances of the risen Jesus, must rest back on an independent source of information, parallel to the Passion narratives in Mark and Luke. How else to account for the *Pedilavium*, the arrest of Jesus, with the connivance of Roman troops, in a garden beyond the wadi Kidron, his appearance before Annas, 'the other disciple', kinsman to the High Priest, who secured Peter's entry into his court, the long trial before the Roman governor, Gabbatha, the trilingual title on the Cross, the seamless robe, the effusion of blood and water from the side of Jesus, and of course the whole dating of events before the Passover?[11] All point in this same direction. While the historicity of this or that item in John's story has been questioned (e.g. his entrustment of his mother to the beloved disciple), and while it is clear that the evangelist has put his own theological stamp on the tradition, many of the episodes we have mentioned have on them the ring of historical truth. Two in particular seem to have a high degree of verisimilitude—the trial before Pilate and the 'rabboni' narrative. All through John's account of the Trial the issue is political, turns on the question of 'kingship', and shows a lively sense of the situation in Judea in the years before the fatal clash between the Romans and the Jews. As for the story of Mary Magdalene's meeting with the risen Jesus in the garden, it has about it something indefinably first-hand which suggests that it never came from the common stock of tradition. 'It stands alone. There is nothing quite like it in the Gospels. Is there anything quite like it in ancient literature?'[12]

What are the practical implications of all this and certain kindred points and consequences to be developed in succeeding chapters?

When our scholars essay to write not a 'life' of Christ (for that is impossible) but a critical and coherent account of his mission and message, it will no longer be good enough to dismiss the fourth gospel with a wave of the hand as a theological document devoid of history. At this point and that they will have to reckon seriously with John's historical testimony. They will not be able to ignore what John has to say about the Baptist and the call of the first disciples. When they undertake to reconstruct the Ministry, they will have to allow for a much longer post-Galilean ministry in the south as well as a pre-Galilean one in Judea. A careful use of the historical tradition underlying John 6, from the Feeding to the Confession, will enable them to make much better sense of the question which Jesus put to his disciples at Caesarea Philippi and the answer which Peter gave. Their account of what happened after Jesus left Galilee and turned southwards will have to make room for a ministry in Perea and a sojourn in Jerusalem from Tabernacles to Dedication. And so on.

When they come to discuss the sayings and teachings of Jesus, they will have to reckon not only with the Johannine parables, the *hypsoun* sayings (which may be more primitive than the synoptic predictions of the Passion and Resurrection) and the predictive sayings in the Farewell Discourses, but also with the possibility that John 6, for example, may well preserve the *substance* of what Jesus said when he was teaching in the Capernaum synagogue, and that the controversies in Jerusalem, recorded in John 7 and 8, may not be so unhistorical as critics have often judged them.

And when they come to describe the last crisis in Jerusalem, they will have to face the fact that John's Passion Story contains a great deal of good history, even if it bears the marks of his own style and his own highly developed sense of drama and occasion.

NOTES

[1] *Christianity according to St John*, p. 17.

[2] *The Theology of the New Testament*, II, p. 3.

[3] *I.F.G.*, p. 449.

[4] *The Background of the New Testament and its Eschatology*, p. 219.

[5] *N.T.S.* July 1959, pp. 246-259.

[6] *N.T.S.* Jan. 1962, pp. 151-154.

[7] *N.T.S.* July 1963, pp. 317-336.

[8] *A.B.S.J.*, xlvii, p. 1.

[9] Dodd, *H.T.F.G.*, p. 292.

[10] If 'Q' had not preserved the great saying about the reciprocal knowledge of the Father and the Son, we should have been tempted to write off similar sayings in the fourth gospel as 'Johannine theologoumena'.

[11] We take St John to be right about the date of the Last Supper, but cannot here go into the pros and cons of the argument. For a lucid discussion, which takes account of Mlle. Jaubert's work, see R. Brown, *New Testament Essays*, pp. 160-7.

[12] C. H. Dodd, *Studies in the Gospels*, p. 20.

5

The Topography of St John

IN 1875 Matthew Arnold,[1] in one of his excursions into Biblical Criticism, declared:

> When St John wants a name for a locality, he takes the first village that comes into his remembrance, without troubling himself whether it suits or no.

Six years later, in his commentary on the fourth gospel, Bishop Westcott[2] held a very different opinion. 'St John,' he wrote, 'speaks of places with an unaffected precision, as familiar in every case with the scene he wishes to recall . . . *he moves about in a country he knows.*'

A generation later Scott Holland[3] took the same view as Westcott. Citing 'Sychar', 'Bethany beyond Jordan', 'Aenon near Salim' and 'Ephraim', he observed that in no case did the site matter.

> These four names serve no intelligible purpose at all except on one hypothesis—that the personal memory of the writer held in it details too small for history to have noted, and that it finds it absolutely impossible to tell its tale without these details of locality emerging.

Consider (he said) such a sentence as John 10.22: 'It was the feast of the Dedication at Jerusalem; it was winter, and Jesus was walking in the temple, in the portico of Solomon.'

> The three viewpoints hang together. In recalling the scene he cannot but recall the place, it was in Solomon's porch; there Jesus had sought shelter from the weather, for it was winter; and the reason they were up in the winter was that it was the Feast of the Dedication, a Maccabaean feast outside the Mosaic regulations. Feast and winter go together, just as Christmas stands to us for winter, or Easter for early spring. The Feast, in this instance, only comes in to explain the cold. And there the whole business ends. Nothing that occurs in the dispute turns on the place, or the weather, or the feast. It is simply jotted down out of memory.

The point is brilliantly made. But through the years that separate Westcott from Scott Holland many scholars had moved away from the view that John the Apostle had any direct connexion with the gospel, as both Westcott and Scott Holland had most definitely held; and, not surprisingly, they tended to 'play down' this argument for apostolic authorship based on the accuracy of John's place-names.

Our question is: How bad, or how good, is his topography? Nearly one hundred years have passed since Arnold and Westcott passed their very different verdicts on it. How stands the case for John's topographical accuracy in the light of modern archaeology?

I

St John's gospel has a dozen place-names not mentioned in the synoptic gospels.

Four of them raise no difficulty at all: Jacob's well (4.6), 'this mountain' (4.20: Gerizim), the Pool of Siloam (9.7), and 'the *wadi* Kidron' (18.1).[4]

Four others cause a little more trouble: Bethany beyond Jordan (1.28), Cana of Galilee (2.1, 4.46), Solomon's portico (10.23), and Ephraim (11.54).

'Bethany beyond (east of) Jordan'[5] has not been located; but this need not surprise us, since in the nature of the case a place used for baptizing would be hard to find long afterwards. But that the chief scene of John's activity was in fact 'beyond Jordan' seems to have been established by T. W. Manson.[6]

Cana is probably Khirbet Qana, nine miles north of Nazareth, where are the ruins of an ancient village.

Nor need we have serious doubts about Solomon's portico. The information given by Josephus[7] makes it tolerably certain that it was on the east side of the colonnaded ambulatory which ran round the outer court of the Temple.

As for Ephraim in 'the country bordering on the desert' (11.54), there seems general agreement that it is to be identified with the modern *Et-Taiyibeh*, lying four miles north-east of Bethel and commanding wonderful views over the Judean desert and the deep 'Rift' of the Jordan valley.

But what of the four remaining place-names: Aenon near Salim, Bethesda, Sychar and Gabbatha?

According to John 3.23f. Jesus came into Judea and baptized, for 'John also was baptizing at Aenon near Salim, because there were many waters there.' The location of Aenon may now be regarded as reasonably certain. Three miles east of Shechem lies the ancient town of Salim of which traces survive in Israelite, Hellenistic and Samaritan literature. And near Salim lies *Ainun* with a name undoubtedly derived from the Aramaic *Ainon* meaning 'little fountain'. Since these two places lie near the head-waters of the *Wadi Far'ah*, with many springs in the vicinity, St John might well declare that 'there were many waters there'.

The next place with a century-long question mark over its accuracy was the Pool of Bethesda in John 5.1. The pool had never been located; and, to make matters worse, the MSS gave here a choice of names: Bethzatha, Belzetha, and Bethsaida, as well as Bethesda. In the last thirty or forty years all this has been dramatically changed. Excavations begun in 1878 by the White Fathers on a site a hundred yards north of the Temple and completed in 1931-32, have laid bare the long-lost pool—or, rather, two quadrilateral pools covering an area of five-thousand square metres, with the upper pool separated from the lower by a wall of rock forming a gangway between them. What remains today is enough to show that porticoes ran round the edge of the double pool and across the gangway in the middle (4 + 1 = 5). As if to make assurance doubly sure, the decipherment of the Copper Scroll from Qumran has independently confirmed the existence of the double pool. Thus the accuracy of John's almost guide-book statement 'There is in Jerusalem, near the sheep-gate, a pool called in Hebrew Bethesda, which has five porticoes' has been vindicated first by the spades of the White Fathers and then, in the last few years, by our experts on the Dead Sea scrolls.[8]

A very old puzzle was the precise locality of Sychar, 'a town of Samaria', with Jacob's well near by. Long ago Jerome[9] declared Sychar and Shechem to be the same, 'Sychar' being a textual error for 'Sychem' (Shechem). Modern scholars were not convinced. Shechem, they thought, was to be identified with Neapolis (Nablus), and, in any case, all good MSS read 'Sychar' at John 4.5. So they identified Sychar with the modern Arab village of *Askar*, a fairly recent settlement, some distance from Jacob's well to the north.

Then, in 1913, some German scholars began excavating the site of Tell Balatah beside Jacob's well; and, as their work proceeded, it became clear that Balatah marked the site of Biblical Shechem. Now 'Shechem' is in fact the reading of the Old Syriac gospels in John 4.5, and though it stands alone, it is to be preferred. The re-

sult is to vindicate Jerome. The town near which Jesus talked to
the Samaritan Woman by Jacob's Well was in fact Sychem alias
Shechem alias Balatah.[10]

Where did Pilate judge Jesus? According to John 19.13 he took
his seat at a place called the Pavement (*Lithostrotos*) and in Aramaic, Gabbatha. This paved court was in the Governor's headquarters or Praetorium. But where was it? At Herod's palace on
the high western hill, or at the Antonia Tower in the north-west
corner of the Temple area? For a long time scholars favoured
Herod's palace. G. A. Smith held this view, as P. Benoit still does.
The chief argument in its favour was the fact that one of Pilate's
successors, Gessius Florus, had his headquarters there in A.D. 65.
'At this time,' wrote Josephus,[11] 'Florus took up his headquarters
at the Palace and on the next day had his tribunal set before it.'
The chief argument against it was the fact that no pavement was
to be found there. Then in the early 'thirties of this century Father
L. H. Vincent's researches decisively re-opened the whole question.
As a result the Antonia Tower, not Herod's palace, became the
likely place of judgment, for Vincent's investigations disclosed, on
the site of the tower, a paved court covering two thousand, five
hundred square yards and standing on a rocky height to which the
name Gabbatha ('ridge', 'elevation') could very properly be applied.

It is true that the Roman Governor could have his headquarters
where he willed, and we cannot be one hundred per cent certain
that Pilate did not stay in Herod's palace in the April of the Crucifixion year. But Vincent's case is very strong. (1) Tradition places
'Pilate's House' near the Antonia Tower. (2) The tower dominating
the Temple area was a much better place to keep an eye on any
possible Jewish insurrection. (3) A pavement which you can see
and walk on—with each stone of it more than a yard square and a
foot thick—is vastly more convincing than any hypothetical courtyard.

Thus archaeological discovery has, at point after point, tended
to confirm John's topography, even if all problems have not been
finally solved. Nor is this all. Most of the place-names peculiar
to the fourth gospel belong to southern Palestine, while northern
place-names found in the synoptics, like Nain, Chorazin, Caesarea
Philippi, and Decapolis, are not found in John. It looks as if the
fourth evangelist's traditions about Jesus were specially associated
with southern Palestine.

II

Your ideal commentator on the fourth gospel, R. D. Potter[12] has written, would not only bring to his study the best resources of modern scholarship; he would also make a full and realistic use of all the data laboriously and loving acquired by those who have lived long in Palestine. Inevitably such men develop what may be called a *Landgefühl*—a sort of sixth sense for appreciating the topographical allusions of the gospel. Four examples will show what he means.

To begin with, let us retrace Jesus' steps as described in John 4.5ff. Journeying up from Judea, he heads north-westwards to the valley of Nablus. His route takes him through 'Sychem' which is the Biblical Shechem, the modern Tell Balatah, and he is about half a mile from it as he reaches Jacob's well, the deepest in the whole of Palestine. When the woman reminds Jesus that 'the well is deep', her remark is almost banal. Sitting by the well, we can feel the force of her 'Our fathers worshipped in this mountain'—can almost see her gesturing towards Gerizim looming up behind her. Not only so, but if it is the right season of the year, we may also see 'the fields white to harvest' on the plain stretching south and east before us. Either John, or his informant, knew that terrain.

Or take the story of the Officer's Son (4.46-54). Jesus is in Cana, the Officer in Capernaum. Examine the lie of the land, and you find that from Khirbet Qana to Tell Hum, the site of the ancient Capernaum, the land drops down from well above sea-level to well below it. At once the thrice-repeated 'down' of the narrative makes obvious sense. 'He begged him to come *down* and heal his son.' 'Sir, come *down* before my child dies.' 'As he was going *down*, his servants met him.'

Consider next the cripple at Bethesda who said to Jesus, 'I have no man to put me into the pool when the water is troubled' (5.7). With the ruins of the long-lost pool of Bethesda now exposed for our inspection and measurement, we can now reconstruct the incident. Four porticoes evidently surrounded the double pool while the fifth stood on the gangway of rock, 6.5 metres wide, separating the two pools. Here the cripple was lying, with other fellow-sufferers. But this is not all. The pool must have been 16 metres deep, with no shallow end. No wonder the cripple had to depend on others to put him into it. He would not only have to be carried there by another but to be held firmly all the time he was in the water.

Or take finally the story of Jesus' trial before Pilate (18-19). Every student of the gospel recalls how John's narrative falls into a series of scenes, alternately outside and inside Pilate's headquarters. Shall we set all this down simply to the dramatic instinct of the evangelist? Possibly, but there is another explanation.

In Book V of his *Jewish Wars* Josephus provides us with an excellent description of the Antonia Fortress on its precipitous rocky site, with its four towers, courtyards, colonnades, etc., and the stairway leading down to the Temple from which the Roman guards could keep watch on it. Now, by combining Josephus's data with Vincent's discoveries, we can make a rough model of the whole lay-out of the Fortress—in the north a rampart and a moat, in the south a palace, in between them the soldiers' quarters, storehouses, stables, etc., and right in the centre (now the basement of the Convent of our Lady of Sion) the great Paved Courtyard, LITHOSTROTOS, 146 feet from east to west and 178 feet from north to south, with its massive flagstones, some scribbled with soldiers' games, still in excellent repair.

With all this in mind we can go back to the gospels, noting from Mark 15.16 that the place of judgment was an *interior* courtyard, and then returning to John 19.13: 'When Pilate heard what they (the Jews) were saying, he brought Jesus out, and took his seat on the tribunal (*bēma*, a portable platform on which the governor's curule chair was placed) at the place known as "The Pavement" (Gabbatha, in the language of the Jews)'.

'It was now early morning,' we read (John 18.28), 'and the Jews stayed outside the headquarters (*praitōrion*) to avoid defilement, so that they could eat the Passover.' There they stood in the vast bays of the entrance to the courtyard. In front of them, on the far side of the courtyard, was the staircase leading into the palace where Pilate was residing; and we can almost see him coming and going between the accusers and the Accused, bringing Jesus into the interior of the palace, and then going out to parley with the Jews before, finally, presenting the Prisoner wearing his thorny crown and clothed in derisive purple, and, at last, condemning Jesus to crucifixion for fear of the exasperated Jews sending a damaging report to the Emperor Tiberius. . . .

Let this evidence for the accuracy of St John's topography suffice.

Did Westcott and Scott Holland, though they wrote long before the discovery of the Pool of Bethesda and the *Lithostrotos*, over-state their case when they said that John 'moved about in a country that he knew' and spoke of its sacred sites with 'unaffected precision'? Did not the evangelist in fact know them in some such way as men—like Dalman and Lagrange and Vincent—who have lived long in Palestine know them today?

Yet, according to good tradition, St John wrote his gospel in far-away Ephesus, perhaps fifty years after the event. Are we not driven to conclude that either John, or an informant of his, had lived at one time in Palestine so that long years after when he wrote his gospel, he was able to include in it first-hand memories of the places where the incarnate Son of God 'manifested his glory' before he 'suffered under Pontius Pilate'?

NOTES

[1] *God and the Bible*, p. 144.

[2] *St John's Gospel*. p. xi. [Italics mine.]

[3] *The Fourth Gospel*, pp. 57f.

[4] St John correctly styles it *cheimarros*, 'wadi', a water-course, full in winter but dry in summer. When Jesus and his disciples crossed it in April, it was probably dry.

[5] Origen, while admitting that the best reading was 'Bethany', himself read 'Bethabara' (the 'fords' of Jordan, Judges 7.24), apparently unable to accept John's view that there were *two* Bethanies. But, by his own confession, he relied on mere hearsay. Bethany beyond Jordan he never discovered because he never went to look. We are therefore entitled to expunge 'Bethabara' from our texts, content to believe that there was a Bethany beyond Jordan, and 'our archaeologists to decide which of the several possible Tells might best correspond' (R. D. Potter in *The Gospels Reconsidered*, p. 93).

[6] *The Servant-Messiah*, p. 40.

[7] *Ant.* XX.ix.7.

[8] On all this see J. Jeremias, *Die Wiederentdeckung von Bethesda* (1949) and his article on the Copper Scroll in the *E.T.* for May 1960. He has also, in my judgment, argued convincingly for the reading 'Bethesda' (so the NEB).

[9] *Quaest. in Genes.* 48.22. P.L. 23,1055.

[10] See W. F. Albright, *The Background of the New Testament and its Eschatology*, p. 160; D. C. Pellett sub 'Sychar' in *The Interpreter's Bible Dictionary*, etc.

[11] Josephus, *Bell. Jud.*, II, 14, 2.

[12] *The Gospels Reconsidered*, p. 90.

6

The Course of the Ministry
in St John

THE fourth evangelist has much to tell about the course of Jesus'
ministry which has apparently no parallel in the first three gospels.
More particularly he describes a pre-Galilean ministry of Jesus in
Judea and a post-Galilean one in Jerusalem and elsewhere. Is St
John here a credible witness, and, if he is, can we use his evidence
to reconstruct the course and shape of Jesus' whole ministry?

We may recall that Renan was decidedly sceptical about St
John's record of the words of Jesus. On his account of the course
of Jesus' ministry, however, he held a quite opposite view. After
declaring that the fourth gospel could not have been written later
than A.D. 100 and that 'there was nothing to prove that the evangelist had any of the synoptics before him when he wrote' (a view
widely held today), he went on:

> The historic background of the Gospel is, to my mind, the life of Jesus
> as it was known among the immediate disciples of Jesus. I must add
> that, in my opinion, this school was better acquainted with the exterior
> circumstances of the life of the Founder than the group whose remem-
> brances constituted the Synoptics. *It had, especially upon the sojourns
> of Jesus at Jerusalem, data which the others did not possess.*[1]

Seventy years later (1933), in another *Life of Jesus*,[2] his fellow-
countryman Maurice Goguel reached similar conclusions, about
'the data which the others did not possess'. These data, viz. the
tradition of a pre-Galilean ministry of Jesus, the extended treatment
given to the Jerusalem ministry, the references to Annas, and the
date of the Last Supper, he believed to be historical. Since Goguel's
time not a few scholars have agreed with him, and recent research
into pre-Johannine tradition has served to confirm this view.

In this chapter, therefore, let us consider St John's record of a pre-Galilean ministry and a post-Galilean one, in order to see whether it is credible.

I

The Pre-Galilean Ministry (John 1-3)

Eusebius[3] preserves a tradition that St John wrote in order to record an early period in Christ's ministry not mentioned by the other evangelists. Was there then a ministry of Jesus in Judea before his Galilean ministry? Concerning what befell between the Temptation in the wilderness and the opening of the Galilean ministry the synoptics tell us nothing directly. The fourth gospel, however, describes a pre-Galilean ministry in Judea. During this time, it says, Jesus called five disciples—Andrew, a nameless one (who may, or may not, have been John, son of Zebedee), Peter, Philip, and Nathanael (not mentioned in the synoptics but traditionally identified with Bartholomew) (1.35-41). Later, after a return to Galilee (1.43-2.12), Jesus visited Jerusalem at Passover time (2.13), cleansed the Temple (2.14-22), talked with Nicodemus (3.1-21) and conducted for a time a ministry in Judea parallel to the Baptist's further north (3.22-30).

St John's early date for the cleansing of the Temple is a notorious difficulty; but, leaving aside the question whether John or Mark is right about this, may we follow John in believing that Jesus found some of his first followers in Judea and conducted a preliminary ministry there before the Galilean one began?

For such a ministry a *prima facie* case can be made out.

(1) The fourth evangelist says there was one. 'For John had not yet been put in prison' (3.24) is the comment he adds to his statement that 'Jesus and his disciples went into the land of Judea' and stayed there baptizing, while the Baptist himself was busy at Aenon by Salim, i.e. probably in eastern Samaria.

(2) Mark's statement 'Now after John was delivered up Jesus came into Galilee preaching the Gospel of God' (1.14; cf. Matt. 4.12, 'Jesus *withdrew* into Galilee') seems to imply some activity of Jesus elsewhere before this.

(3) There are several hints in the synoptics themselves which almost compel us to believe that Jesus had made an appeal to the people of Jerusalem and Judea before he made his last fateful journey to the capital. Most important of these is Jesus' lament, 'O

Jerusalem, Jerusalem . . . how often would I have gathered your children together . . . and you would not!' (Luke 13.34; Matt. 23.37). Further, the ready response of the Galilean fishermen to Jesus' call to 'become fishers of men' (Mark 1.16-20) makes much more sense if, as St John says, they had some previous knowledge of Jesus before they left all and followed him.

This *prima facie* case can be further strengthened by an analysis of the contents of John 1.35-51 (the call of the first disciples) and 3.22-30 (the concurrent ministries).

1.35-51

While this section owes much to the evangelist, it yields four pieces of evidence which suggest that St John is here making use of early tradition which did not come from the synoptics and may even have had Aramaic roots.

(i) The statement which makes some of Jesus' disciples come over from the Baptist instead of being called in Galilee.

(ii) The suggestion of an original group of *five* disciples. This finds independent confirmation in, of all places, the Talmud. 'Jesus,' says a *baraita* (i.e. a Jewish tradition from the tannaitic period) 'had five disciples.'

(iii) The naming of Peter (40-42). Here only in the four gospels is he called by his Aramaic name Kephas. Further, he is 'Simon, son of John' (not 'Jonah', as in Matt. 16.17), a version of Peter's patronymic independently attested in the *Gospel to the Hebrews*.

(iv) The statement that Peter and Andrew as well as Philip were 'Bethsaidans' (44). Mark 1.29-31 would lead us to infer that Capernaum was the home of Peter and Andrew.

Thus encouraged by facts which suggest that St John had independent and, so far as we can judge, reliable evidence about the original followers of Jesus, we may proceed to study his account of Jesus' ministry in Judea.

3.22-30

This is our main evidence for the early Judean ministry of Jesus.

Now it can be shown by careful analysis[4] that most of it is not the evangelist's creation but derives from pre-Johannine tradition. To be sure, the evangelist's hand can be traced in the comment of v. 24 (already discussed) and probably in v. 27 ('No one can receive anything except what is given him from above'). For the rest, we may regard as 'traditional':

22. ('Jesus and his disciples went into the land of Judea.') This is one of several 'travel traditions' to be found in the gospel; we shall find some more in John 7-10.

23. ('John also was baptizing at Aenon near Salim, etc.'); a 'traditional' piece of topography whose accuracy Albright[5] seems to have vindicated.

25. ('Now a discussion arose between John's disciples and a Jew over purifying.') This is a detached note of high historical value. The Greek word *katharismos* suggests a reference to the various Jewish rites of lustration. It is no wild guess that the disputant may have come from the Qumran community.

26-30. This is a 'pronouncement story' resembling many in the synoptics. It contains an implied question (26), a comment by the Baptist which may be 'traditional' (28), the parable of the Bridegroom and the Best Man (29) and an appended aphorism (30, 'He must increase, but I must decrease') which is not unlike similar things in the synoptics.

A point of interest is that this pre-Johannine tradition declares that Jesus himself baptized (cf. the qualifying remark in 4.2). But for our purpose the chief value of this analysis is that the passage is shown to preserve pre-Johannine tradition concerning a ministry of Jesus in the south, before he came into Galilee. There is a gap, as K. L. Schmidt[6] observed, between Mark 1.13 and 14 in which there is room for the special tradition on which St John drew. We need not hesitate to fill it with the traditional material we have been studying. The general probability of a preliminary Judean ministry of Jesus, we may fairly claim, has been established. Of its nature and length we can of course say little except that it must have been a time of preparation for a wider ministry. That it was successful, St John tells us, declaring that it was the Pharisees' jealousy of Jesus' success which made Jesus move northwards, via Samaria, into Galilee (4.1ff.). That Jesus and John the Baptist eventually moved apart is certain; for the theory that there was a break between them due to ill-feeling there is not a scrap of evidence. For the sequel to all this we have to turn from St John to St Mark. Mark 1.14 suggests that the interval was broken by Jesus' receipt of news that the Baptist had been cast into prison. 'After John was delivered up,'[7] he says, 'Jesus came into Galilee preaching the

Gospel of God.' The tidings of Herod's imprisonment of the Baptist seems to have been the signal for which Jesus was waiting. The forerunner had run his course. It was now time for the Mightier One to appear, with 'news' which far transcended John's.

II

The Post-Galilean Ministry (John 7-11)

As St John testifies to a preliminary ministry of Jesus in Judea, so in chapters 7-11 he testifies to a later one in the south. Can we accept his testimony?

Sixty years ago—in this country at any rate—when it was still possible to regard the fourth gospel as based on real history, and not simply a theological document sitting very loose to historical events, the greatest of then living British New Testament scholars, William Sanday of Oxford, wrote thus about the chapters now before us: [8]

> The historical value of the Fourth Gospel comes out strongly in this period. Rarely has any situation been described with the *extraordinary vividness* and truth to fact of chapter 7 (see esp. vv. 11-15, 25-27, 31, 32, 40-52). Not less graphic are the details of chapter 9; and there is *marked precision* in the statements of John 10.22f., 40f., 11.45-57. We note a special intimacy with what passes in the inner councils of the Sanhedrin (John 7.47-52, 11.47-53). This intimate knowledge might have been derived through Nicodemus or through the connexion hinted at in 18.15. But, apart from the *peculiar verisimilitude* of these details, some such activity as that described in these chapters is required to explain the great catastrophe which followed. It is impossible that Jesus should have been so much a stranger to Judea and Jerusalem as the Synoptic narrative would at first sight seem to make him. For the steps which lead up to the end we must go to St John.

This is a very just evaluation of the chapters in question, and much different from the view of the historical worth of St John fashionable during the last few decades, especially among radical New Testament scholars like Bultmann[9] and his followers. But 'the flight from history' (into existentialism) which has characterized so much modern New Testament scholarship now shows signs of coming to an end as a saner and truer view of the historicity not of the synoptics alone but of St John also takes its place. Here we are only concerned to insist that it is unjustifiable prejudice against finding genuine historical tradition in the most theological of the gospels which has led critics to ignore the passages cited by Sanday, or imagine that the evangelist has created them all *ex nihilo*. Unless the reader has a quite incurable bias against the historical value of the fourth gospel, he must admit that a great deal here is very vivid and self-authenticating. Now among these passages we find six notes about Jesus' movements after the Galilean ministry was over:

7.10 Jesus went up to Jerusalem at the Feast of Tabernacles, i.e. in the autumn.

10.22f. Jesus was teaching in Solomon's portico at the Feast of Dedication, i.e. about the winter solstice.

10.40 Jesus crossed the Jordan into Perea—in fact to 'Bethany beyond Jordan', the original locus of the Baptist's mission (1.23).

11.17 Jesus travelled from there to Bethany in Judea.

11.54 Because of growing hostility Jesus retired with his disciples to Ephraim and 'the country bordering on the desert'.

12.1 Six days before the Passover Jesus returned to Bethany and, the day after, entered Jerusalem.

Let us comment on some of these notes of movement.

The journeying implied in John 7.10 and 10.40 is probably the same as that implied in Mark 10.1. There we learn that Jesus 'went into the territories of Judea and Transjordan'. This looks like an 'undesigned coincidence' between John and Mark.

The reference to the Feast of Dedication (10.22f.), with its vivid description of Jesus teaching, during wintry weather, in Solomon's portico strongly suggests the reminiscence of an eye-witness.

The story of Jesus' movement across Jordan to the other Bethany where the Baptist had originally baptized (10.40; cf. 1.23) is probably another 'travel tradition'.

We do not know where precisely the town of Ephraim named in 11.54 was. But this, so far from telling against the historical value of the reference, in fact rather favours it. The author writing years later in Ephesus could hardly be expected to be interested in an obscure Palestinian town.

Finally, when St John records that the Anointing at Bethany took place six days before the Passover, i.e. on the Saturday before Palm Sunday (12.1), he is probably to be trusted. Mark's dating of the event is very vague; and since he appears to have interpolated the story of the Anointing between 14.1f. (the priests' plot) and 14.10f. (the treachery of Judas), many commentators think John's date is right.

On the basis of this evidence Goguel[10] suggests the following account of Jesus' movements during the last phase of his ministry:

(a) Jesus left Galilee and went up to the feast of Tabernacles (autumn)—John 7.10.

(b) There he taught for three months until the feast of Dedication (*Hanukkah*—about the winter solstice)—John 10.22.

(c) Soon after, because of mounting hostility, Jesus went to Transjordan, i.e. Perea—John 10.40.

(d) Six days before the Passover, i.e. about the beginning of April, he returned to Jerusalem—John 12.1f.

This view has commended itself to many. If Goguel is right, the fourth gospel implies a period of *six months*, including a three months' ministry in Jerusalem, between Jesus' departure from Galilee and the final Passover.

Can this be reconciled with Mark's account? *Prima facie*, the answer is No. After Jesus leaves Galilee, so swiftly does Mark's narrative move that we readily imagine that events followed hot-foot on each other and that *a week* saw the life of Jesus end in the ignominy of the Cross. Did things really happen as quickly as this?

In an important article T. W. Manson[11] argued that, if we study Mark's narrative carefully, we shall find that the events related in Mark 10-16 occupied at least *six months*.

The first passage worthy of attention is Mark 10.1: 'He came into the territories of Judah and Transjordan and there came to him crowds and again he *taught them*.' If we have regarded this verse as recording simply a journey to the south with some incidental teaching included, we had better think again. It is in fact the record of a *ministry* in Judea—including presumably Jerusalem —and Perea, with different groups of people receiving instruction from the Lord.

Consider first the historicity of the Perean ministry. Both Mark and John testify to it (John 10.40f. asserting that Jesus won 'many' followers in Perea). Moreover Perea was part of Antipas's dominions and there are sound reasons[12] for thinking that the Baptist had his headquarters there. If, as we have seen reason to believe, Jesus had earlier been associated with the Baptist, he would be returning to familiar ground in 'Bethany beyond Jordan'. Certainly his fame had already travelled to Perea, since we are told that some of the crowds who heard him preach in Galilee came from Transjordan (Mark 3.8). In short, the ministry in Perea looks like fact, not fiction.

Now let us return to John's record of a three months' ministry in Jerusalem before the departure to Perea, in order to see whether Mark's account permits or precludes it.

To begin with, we must remember that even in Mark there are *hints* of a Jerusalem ministry lasting much longer than a week. This is the clear implication of what Jesus said to the arresting posse in Gethsemane, 'Day after day I was with you in the temple teaching' (Mark 14.49).

Second: scholars have long felt that the controversies in Jerusalem between Jesus and the Jewish authorities, recorded in Mark 11 and 12, cannot all have occurred on one crowded day in Passion Week, but must rather belong to the 'day after day' activity of Jesus in the temple and its precincts.

Third: closer study of Mark 11-13, i.e. his account of the Jerusalem ministry, points to the same conclusion.[13]

In Mark 11.1-25 the narratives are set in a framework of three days, 11.1, 11.12 and 11.19f.; and apparently all that is recorded in 11.27-13.37 took place on the *third* of these days. But this arrangement is patently artificial, for (1) the third day is absurdly overloaded, (2) Mark 13 (the apocalyptic discourse) is a composite document, and (3) most of the 'conflict stories' in 11 and 12 probably form a pre-Markan complex which Mark fitted in here because the first of them ('by what authority?') had its right historical context here.

Mark has therefore imposed on 11-13 a chronological scheme to harmonize it with the Passion narrative (14-16) so as to describe in detail the successive days of the last week. To this we may add that at 14.1 comes the Passion story proper with a fresh note of time and a reference to the Jewish calendar: 'It was now two days before the Passover and the feast of Unleavened Bread.' This is a new start: there is no chronological connexion with what goes before. In other words, the course of events in Mark 11-13 has been much *telescoped*, and it is absurd to suppose that everything from the triumphal entry to the finding of the empty tomb happened in one week.

When now we turn back from St Mark to St John, we find in John 7-10 an account of controversies in Jerusalem between Jesus and the Jews which lasted over a period of three months. If 'probability is the guide of life', we must judge St John's three months a much likelier length of time for all that happened than the day or two suggested by a superficial reading of St Mark.

In the light of this discussion the Johannine record of the Jerusalem ministry takes on a new aspect of authenticity. A good deal of it is taken up with the question of Jesus' authority and his Messiahship. This is altogether probable. Two of the Jerusalem controversies which Mark records concern Messiah's Davidic sonship and Jesus' authority for acting as he did (Mark 12.35-37 and 11.27-33); and it is highly significant that they have equivalents in John's account of the Jerusalem ministry (7.14-18 and 40-44). The question 'By what authority are you doing these things?' is connected in Mark with the Cleansing of the Temple. This, as we have suggested, is probably right historically; and it is likely that it was during the three months' ministry in Jerusalem (whether at Tabernacles or at the Dedication festival) that Jesus cleansed the Temple. Finally, it is worth noting that, if St John relates that Jesus taught 'in the treasury' (8.20), we have a parallel in Mark 12.41. In fine, most of what St Mark tells in 11.15-12.44 is readily intelligible against the background of the three months' Jerusalem ministry recorded by John.

We have argued that there is a time gap between the events recorded in Mark 11-13 and Mark 14.1, i.e. between the clashes with the Jerusalem authorities and the last Passover of Jesus' ministry. This gap St John fills with (*a*) a brief reference to Jesus' Perean ministry, (*b*) the story of his return to Bethany and the raising of Lazarus which, he says, fatally sharpened the conflict between Jesus and the Sanhedrin, and (*c*) an account of Jesus' retreat from Jerusalem north-eastwards to Ephraim on the edge of the desert country. All this took about three months and culminated in Jesus returning from Ephraim to Jerusalem about Passover time in order to finish the work his Father had given him to do.

III

It is the opinion of many good modern authorities[14] that the public ministry of Jesus lasted between two and three years, and that the Crucifixion took place in the April of A.D. 30. Using St John's chronological data as framework and fitting the Galilean ministry into it between John 5-7, we suggest the following scheme of dates and events:

A.D. 27—Baptist's mission and Jesus' early Judean ministry.
Spring A.D. 28 to Spring A.D. 29—the Galilean ministry.

October A.D. 29 to December A.D. 29—the Jerusalem ministry.
January to March, A.D. 30—Jesus in Perea and Ephraim.
April A.D. 30—return to Jerusalem and Crucifixion.

NOTES

[1] *The Life of Jesus*, pp. 18f. [Italics mine.]

[2] *The Life of Jesus*, pp. 150-7, 405-25.

[3] *H.E.*, III, p. 27.

[4] Dodd, *H.T.F.G.*, pp. 278-287.

[5] *The Background of the New Testament*, etc., p. 159. See also C. Scobie, *John the Baptist*, pp. 163f.

[6] *Der Rahmen der Geschichte Jesu*, p. 34.

[7] *Paradothēnai* probably means not 'arrested' but 'delivered up' in accordance with God's purpose.

[8] *Outlines of the Life of Christ* (1905), p. 131. [Italics mine.]

[9] See e.g. Bultmann's *Jesus and the Word*, p. 12, for his *tout court* dismissal of John as a source.

[10] *The Life of Jesus*, pp. 238-250, 401-28.

[11] *B.J.R.L.*, xxxiii (1951) 'The Cleansing of the Temple', pp. 271-82.

[12] (a) John 1.28 puts the Baptist's original activity on the far side of the Jordan; (b) Luke 3.3 says that the Baptist preached all around the Jordan valley; (c) Herod Antipas, who executed him, ruled not over Judea but over Galilee and Perea and shut John up finally in Machaerus in Perea.

[13] V. Taylor, *The Gospel according to St Mark*, p. 450; C. E. B. Cranfield, *St Mark*, p. 347.

[14] E.g. G. B. Caird, *The Interpreter's Bible Dictionary*, I, pp. 599ff.

7

The Miracles in St John

THAT there are distinct differences between St John's record and treatment of Jesus' miracles and that found in the synoptics every serious student of the New Testament knows. But how deep do they go? Are they differences of kind or only of emphasis? And what is the place and purpose of miracle in the Johannine Story of Jesus?

It is usually said that St John records seven miracles: Water into Wine (2), the healing of the Officer's Son (4), the cure of the Bethesda Cripple (5), the Feeding of the Five Thousand (6), the Walking on the Water (6), the healing of the Man born Blind (9) and the raising of Lazarus (11).

But it is far from certain that John 6.16-21 implies a miracle: the crucial phrase *peripatounta epi tēs thalassēs* would naturally mean 'walking by the sea' (cf. 21.1, where *epi tēs thalassēs* does mean 'by the sea'); and it may well be that 'it is the recognition of Jesus, unexpectedly present to the disciples in their need, that is the true centre of the story'.[1]

Two further points may be added: (1) Two of the Johannine miracles—the healing of the Officer's Son and the Feeding of the Five Thousand—occur also in the synoptic tradition, though St John did not derive them thence. (2) Unlike the synoptics, John records no exorcisms.

That there are so few miracles in John is in line with the evangelist's express purpose. Jesus, he tells us (20.30f.), did perform 'many more signs': the six (or seven) he has narrated were specially chosen to foster saving faith in Jesus among his readers.

Nonetheless this is the first main difference between St John and the synoptics in the matter of miracle. In Mark, for example, 209 verses out of a total 661 deal with miracle, i.e. 31 per cent. John's twenty chapters contain no more than six or seven miracles.

Different also is John's vocabulary for miracle. In the synoptics miracles are *dunameis*, 'acts of power', 'mighty works'. In St John they are *erga*, 'works', when Jesus is speaking, and when the evangelist or others are speaking, *sēmeia*, 'signs', i.e. acts symbolic of spiritual truth. The old definition of a 'sign' was 'a wonder with a meaning in it'; and St John, as every student knows, likes to draw out the spiritual meaning of Jesus' miracles. Later we shall discuss the Old Testament background of these two Johannine terms for miracle; meantime we note that, whereas for St John 'sign' is mostly a favourable term for miracle, in the synoptic tradition it is definitely a 'bad' word. There it means some thaumaturgical *tour de force*—a visible manifestation of overmastering power which, so to speak, would write the truth of Jesus' claims plain against the sky. And this kind of proof or sign, as we know, Jesus steadfastly refused to give when the Pharisees and others asked for it. 'No sign shall be given this generation,' he said (Mark 8.12); and again, 'No sign shall be given it except the sign of Jonah'— the sign, that is, which consisted in himself and his message, as in the Old Testament story of Jonah and Nineveh (Luke 11.29f.; Matt. 12.38f.).

A third difference concerns what we may call context. In the synoptics, as we shall emphasize presently, the context of all Jesus' miracles is his proclamation of the coming of the Kingdom of God. When we turn to St John, we find this phrase only twice (John 3.3, 5): in this gospel Jesus' 'signs' manifest the glory of God or of his Son (2.11, 11.4, 40).

A final difference between St John and the synoptics concerns their theological treatment of the miracles. In the synoptics the theological, or symbolic, import of the miracle does not often lie on the surface. But we have only to consider stories like the healings of the Centurion's Son or the Syro-Phoenician Woman's Daughter to see that it is there. In St John, on the other hand, a 'work' of Jesus is commonly accompanied, or followed, by a 'word' explicating its spiritual meaning, so that it sometimes seems as if the evangelist were using the miracle as a text for a theological sermon. Thus the Feeding of the Five Thousand is interpreted in the great discourse on the Bread of Life; the cure of the Man born Blind serves to set Christ forth as 'the light of the world' and to

typify what is going on in the realm of spiritual enlightenment; and
the raising of Lazarus proclaims Christ as the source of life—
eternal life, life over which physical death has no power—'I am
the resurrection and the life'.

How radical are all these differences between St John and the
synoptics? In order to see them in true perspective, it will be well
to remind ourselves what place and purpose the miracles have in
the ministry of Jesus as recorded in the first three gospels.

II

We have already noted how large miracle bulks in the synoptics.
This is not so surprising when we remember that Jesus' 'mighty
works' are there presented as an integral part of his total message
or proclamation. But in what sense?

Nowadays there survive few champions of the traditional view
that the mighty works of Jesus were meant to serve an *evidential*
purpose, i.e. to prove his heavenly origin and accredit him as the
divine Son of God. This view (which we associate with William
Paley's famous book,[2] though it is much older) is seen to be open
to fatal objections. (1) Jesus did not perform miracles in order to
call attention to his credentials. The Temptation narrative shows
that right at the outset of his ministry Jesus had resolved that God's
Messiah should not rely on what we might call 'stunts', in order to
attract a following, and later, as we have seen, he refused all re-
quests for 'signs'. (2) Such a view does serious violence to the close
connexion between miracle and faith (a point to be discussed presently). (3) It portrays Jesus as a kind of heavenly bell-man calling
attention to his divinity by his miracles—which is strangely out
of keeping with one of whom it was written that he should not
strive, or cry, or make his voice heard in the streets (Matt. 12.19).

But if in the synoptics Jesus' mighty works were not signs in this
spectacular sense, they were signs in another sense—for those who
had eyes to see—*Gesta Christi*, works of the Messiah (Matt. 11.2)
and tokens of the inbreaking New Age.

Today scholars agree that the whole burden of Jesus' preaching
was the Kingdom of God and its coming. The Kingdom, or Reign,
of God—an eschatological concept—signifies the sovereign activity
of God in saving men and overcoming evil and the New Order of
things thus established. Now it was the very heart of Jesus' 'good
news' that this New Order was no longer a shining hope on the

far horizon but, in some sense, a present reality in his person and ministry. And for Jesus, as the synoptics indicate, his mighty works were signs of that Kingdom's coming and presence. They were tokens of the New Age in which the power of the living God was at work through his Messiah in hitherto unknown ways—encountering and defeating evil and the devil, whether it was the demonic distortion of a man's personality, or the assault of disease on his natural vitality and vigour, or the foretaste of death, 'the last enemy'. In one phrase, the mighty works of Jesus were *the Kingdom of God in action*, and an integral part of his message. If by word and parable he announced the advent of this Kingdom and challenged men to accept his 'good news' as true, his extraordinary deeds were signs for those who had eyes to see that God's saving Rule was among them, and he was visiting and redeeming his people. 'If I by the finger of God cast out devils,' he told his critics, 'then the kingdom of God has come upon you' (Luke 11.20; Matt. 12.28). 'Heal the sick,' he commanded his apostolic missioners, 'and say to them, The Kingdom of God has come near you' (Luke 10.9; Matt. 10.7f.).

Consider one further aspect of this dynamic revelation of the Kingdom: Jesus saw his miracles as *the fulfilment of Old Testament Messianic prophecy*. When the imprisoned Baptist sent his messengers to ask him, 'Art thou he that should come?' Jesus replied, 'Go and tell John what you have seen and heard: the blind receive sight, the lame walk, lepers are cleansed, and the deaf hear, the dead are raised up, the poor have good news preached to them. And blessed is he who takes no offence at me' (Luke 7.20ff.; Matt. 11.4-6, echoing Isa. 29.18f., 35.5f., 61.1). In the same tenor he congratulated his disciples, 'Blessed are the eyes which see what you see! For I tell you that many prophets and kings desired to see what you see, and did not see it, and to hear what you hear, and did not hear it' (Luke 10.23f.; Matt. 13.16f.). As in his answer to the Baptist, the 'things seen' must be the miracles. What the prophets and kings had vainly yearned to see and hear, what the disciples were now seeing and hearing, was the advent of the Kingdom in both work and word.

III

If this is a true account of the synoptic miracles, we may go on to make comparisons with St John's.

But, before we do this, let us recall that in the fourth gospel Jesus' own word for miracle is not 'sign' but 'work' (*ergon*). Eighteen times he uses it to describe his Father's work or the work his Father has given him to do. (In point of fact, the concept of 'work' is wider than that of miracle, for Jesus can apply the term to his whole ministry, as in 17.4; but, generally, the reference is to his miracles.) This term takes us back to the Old Testament concept of God's 'works', whether in creation or in redemptive history (Gen. 2.2; Ex. 34.10; Ps. 66.5; etc.). By calling his miracles 'works' Jesus is associating his ministry with the creative and saving works of his Father in the past (but not in the past only: 'My Father,' he says (5.17) 'has never yet ceased his work, and I am working too').

The word the evangelist and others use to describe Jesus' miracles is 'signs' (*sēmeia*).[3] Here again the Old Testament supplies the background. More particularly, we recall the 'signs' which God wrought for his people at the Exodus from Egypt. Exodus motifs abound in St John;[4] and if the evangelist held, as he did, that Jesus had replaced, and superseded, so many of the gifts and institutions of the Exodus, it was no long step to regard Jesus' miracles as signs corresponding to those by which God had delivered old Israel.[5]

In the LXX the Greek *sēmeion* is the normal rendering of the Hebrew *ōth*; and when we study St John's concept of 'sign', it is the *ōth*, or symbolic act, of the Hebrew prophet which provides the best key to what he means. The *ōth* of the prophet was both picture and pledge—not only an acted parable but a real earnest of what God was bringing to pass. (Thus, to take one example, from Jeremiah 19, when the prophet broke his pitcher in the valley of Hinnom, his act was not only a dramatic representation of the impending ruin of Jerusalem; it was a little part of the reality yet unseen as a whole, i.e. it helped to accomplish what it symbolized.[6]) So in John's gospel Jesus' signs are pictures and pledges of the New Order which God is inaugurating through him. The Feeding of the Five Thousand, to cite one instance only, is not merely a wonderful act of compassion, it is a picture and pledge of Christ giving himself for the life and nourishment of mankind.

Once we realize this, the disappearance from John of the Kingdom-of-God setting for Jesus' miracles loses any real significance. If the Jewish phrase 'kingdom of God' occurs in only one passage (3.3-5), the reality it connotes is expressed in various ways in John's gospel, most notably in terms of 'eternal life' conceived as a present possibility and blessing. In other words, the miracles of Jesus, whether in the synoptics or in St John, are tokens of what we nowadays call 'inaugurated eschatology'—the advent of God's saving sovereignty among men in the mission of Jesus. In St John the miracles reveal not the 'kingdom' but the 'glory' of God; but when we grasp that by 'the glory of God' is meant 'the revelation of God's presence among men in saving action',[7] the difference is seen to be one merely of wording.

Having discussed the various words for miracle and shown that in the synoptics and St John Jesus' miracles are signs of the salvation God is bringing through his Messiah, we may now note that the six Johannine miracles are basically of the same type and kind as we find in the synoptics. Four are miracles of healing—the Officer's Son, the Bethesda Cripple, the Man born Blind, and the raising of Lazarus. Two—Water into Wine and the Feeding of the Five Thousand—are nature miracles, though it is fair to point out that the New Testament does not make our distinction between healing and nature miracles.

A charge often levelled against St John is that he has enhanced the miraculous element in the gospel story. Does he not tell of a hundred and twenty gallons of water turned into wine, of a cripple healed after thirty-eight years of disablement, of a man restored to life after he had been four days dead? But this is only one side of the medal. On the other side, St John greatly reduces the number of miracles (whereas Matthew and Luke tend to increase what they found in Mark); he omits the references to wonder-struck awe in the beholders and the excited reports of the bystanders which characterize the synoptic miracle-stories; and in one case—Walking on the Water—he appears to 'de-miraculize' the miraculous.

We may summarize our findings so far by saying that, though St John does not present Jesus' miracles in the Kingdom-of-God setting found in the synoptics, this is merely a matter of terminology; both the synoptics and St John record the same general type of miracle, and both agree in regarding them as an integral part of Jesus' ministry and as manifestations of the power and pity of God in decisive action for man's salvation.

Even the apparent discrepancy between the synoptics and St John on miracles as 'signs' is not so real as might appear. On the one hand, the Johannine Jesus deprecates the dependence of faith

on signs: 'Except you see signs and wonders, you will not believe'
(4.48): a saying with a synoptic ring about it. Jesus is distinguish-
ing between faith founded on mere wonder-working and faith based
on a spiritual understanding of the sign. On the other, the synoptic
Jesus replies to the Baptist's question by appealing to his mighty
works: 'Go and tell John what you have seen and heard.' That
is, he allows a place for his miracles in the establishment of faith
(cf. John 5.36).

To this question of the relation between *faith and miracle* in the
synoptics and John we now turn.

It has been said of Jesus' miracles that faith is the sphere in
which God's power comes to fruition. And certainly in the synoptic miracle stories an appeal to faith on the part of the person to
be healed is a regular feature. We need not quote all Jesus' appeals:
What we may usefully note is (*a*) the demand Jesus often makes
for the patient's *co-operation* in a cure, as seen in his various commands to the sick and diseased: 'Rise, pick up your bed and walk',
'Stretch forth your hand', 'Go and show yourself to the priests',
etc; and (*b*) the sheer *pertinacity* of the people who desire a cure
for themselves or those they represent, whether it be the friends
of the paralytic, the Woman with the Issue, or blind Bartimaeus.
In such cases faith is 'an energetic and importunate grasping after
God's help'[8] as it is present in Jesus.

When we turn to discover what faith means in the fourth gospel,
the first surprise awaiting us is that the noun 'faith' does not occur
at all. Instead we have the verb 'believe' almost a hundred times.[9]
This can only mean that for St John true faith was essentially
something energetic and active. Next, we note in the story of the
Bethesda Cripple that faith is no mere pale and passive belief. 'Have
you the will to health?' Jesus asks him, indicating that this will
to health is part of what he means by faith. We may compare John
9.7 where Jesus orders the man born blind to prove his faith by
co-operative action, 'Go and wash in the pool of Siloam.'

If, probing deeper into what St John means by true faith, we
ask, What is the proper response to Jesus' signs? we get a clearer
idea of what is meant. Some people like the Pharisees (9.41) and
Caiaphas (11.47) see or hear of Jesus' signs with no faith at all.
Others like the Jerusalemites (2.23ff.) or Nicodemus (3.2) are evidently prepared to regard Jesus as a wonder-worker sent by God.
But this is not for Jesus real faith. The one right response is that

of those who see what is signified by Jesus' signs, divine who he
is, and commit themselves to him. Among such are the Officer
whose son was healed, the Man born blind, and of course Peter and
the disciple-band (6.69).

In St John's gospel, therefore, more clearly than in the synoptics,
faith is distinguished from mere trust in a wonder-worker; but,
fundamentally, in the emphasis laid on faith as the necessary
accompaniment of miracle, the Jesus of St John is at one with
the synoptic Jesus.

We may sum up our conclusions about the Johannine miracles
in relation to the synoptic ones in four statements:

First: In John we have fewer miracles (with no exorcisms), plus
a different vocabulary for them.

Second: In both the synoptics and the fourth gospel miracles
are not evidential *addenda* to Jesus' preaching, but an essential
part of God's (eschatological) saving activity in Jesus the Messiah.

Third: In the fourth gospel we find much more emphasis on the
theological, or symbolic, aspect of the miracles. In the synoptics,
the didactic element is there, but it is secondary. In St John it is
primary.

Fourth: For both the synoptics and St John, faith is an active
accompaniment of miracle; but St John more clearly distinguishes
it from mere trust in a wonder-worker. (Jesus prefers faith without
signs but concedes the usefulness of 'works' for the weaker in faith
(John 10.38, 14.11).)

Thus there are differences, but they are differences essentially of
emphasis.

IV

Now let us say something about the problem of history as it concerns St John's record of the miracles of Jesus.

St John, as we have seen, is at great pains to bring out the theological or symbolic meaning of Jesus' miracles. But if this is so,
can the historical details in his miracle-stories be relied on? Can
his kind of theological approach exist side by side with an interest
in true history?

Here of course we touch on the bigger question of what historiography—the art of writing history—really is.[10] In the nineteenth
century, when so-called 'scientific history' was the order of the
day, men believed that the historian's main business was, by

eschewing all interpretation, to establish the naked facts, and that the earliest account of an event was necessarily truer than a later one. This concept of historiography is now seriously called in question. Nowadays we are coming to see that history is never the uninterpreted account of bare facts. What we used to call 'facts' are really interpretations of evidence, and no historian is unbiassed, comes to his task without presuppositions—since, inevitably, he is conditioned by 'the climate of opinion', the assumptions of his milieu, the kind of man he is. Moreover, most of us would now admit that contemporary evidence can be vitiated and that events (whether it be the mission of Jesus or the life of Bismarck) need to be seen 'in the long perspective of history' (as we say) if their true significance is to be appraised.

All this has its bearing on St John and history. If history is indeed the unbiassed chronicle of bare events, St John has no claim to be a writer of history. If the truest historical account of an event is that written nearest in time to the event itself, John's gospel written, say, half a century after the ministry of Jesus, is at a grave disadvantage. But if all so-called 'bare facts' are interpreted facts, and some interpretations are truer than others, and if it does not follow that earlier accounts are necessarily truer than later ones, then St John cannot be disqualified *tout court* as a witness to historical truth.

Our immediate question, however, is this: Would a writer like St John, with a declared interest in the theological or symbolic meaning of Jesus' miracles, really have worried about historical veracity and accuracy?

Now clearly we can have symbolic representation without concern for historical truth. Allegory is often in this category. But there are three good reasons for holding that St John was not a symbolist or allegorist of this kind.

First: St John's central thesis is that 'the Word became flesh'. He held that eternal reality had been conclusively and finally revealed in a historical Person who had lived, suffered, died and risen again. The narrative he unfolded was, therefore, not just a vehicle for the exposition of symbolic truths. It was of capital importance to him that what he narrated had actually happened and had been seen by eye-witnesses.[11]

Second: the whole trend of recent research into his gospel has been to show how much good and independent historical tradition underlies St John's record of the Story of Jesus. This has been a main point in most of this book, and we need not dwell on it further now.

Third : the details in St John's miracle-stories hardly suggest that the evangelist is deliberately creating narratives for symbolic purposes.[12] The healing of the Officer's Son takes place soon after Jesus moved from Judea to Galilee (4.43f.); the thrice-repeated 'down' (from Cana to Capernaum) of his narrative shows topographical truth; and after the miracle, St John records that Jesus went up to Jerusalem for one of the Jewish festivals. Modern archaeological research has vindicated the accuracy of what St John has to tell us about the Pool of Bethesda (5.1ff.), and we note that, according to the evangelist, the cripple was cured on a sabbath. We have shown in another chapter that St John's narrative of the Feeding and its sequel has a fair claim to be considered more historical than that found in Mark 6-8. If the timing and place of the healing of the man born blind is less specific, John 9.1 suggests that Jesus was passing along a road from the Temple on the last day of the festival of Tabernacles, and the Pool of Siloam is mentioned (9.7). The raising of Lazarus is said to have taken place at Bethany which is 'near Jerusalem, about two miles off' (11.18); immediately after it Jesus is recorded to have journeyed to Ephraim in 'the country bordering on the desert' (11.54); and once again a Jewish feast, the Passover, is said to be imminent. Such details do not suggest that St John invented them as *mise-en-scène* for his symbolism; rather they leave the impression of actual events and places to which St John has come to accord a special significance. In short, his intention was to narrate what actually happened.

From the question of historicity let us turn last to the related one of credibility.

The stories of the healings of the Officer's Son, the Bethesda Cripple and the Man born Blind should raise no insuperable difficulties for Christian faith. When so sceptical a critic as Bultmann[13] concedes that 'Jesus did undoubtedly heal the sick and cast out demons', who are we to demur?

Much more perplexing for the modern Christian are the Sign at Cana, the Feeding of the Five Thousand and the raising of Lazarus.

In the light of what we have said about St John and history we may well believe that John 2.1-12 is based on an actual historical situation at which Jesus somehow 'saved the situation' for a village wedding party. The trouble is that the provision of one hundred and twenty gallons of wine when men had already 'drunk freely' is not an act of human prudence, still less of Divine Providence. This consideration, the synoptic parable of the New Wine in the old wine-skins (Mark 2.22), and the position of the story at the opening of the ministry of Jesus, suggest that St John is giving us here a dominant theme of his gospel. Jewish legalism symbolized by the six water-pots for purification becomes the wine which gladdens the marriage-feast of the Kingdom of God. In this sign Jesus is saying in effect, 'This is the meaning of my whole ministry: it is a changing of water into wine.'

As for the Feeding, two possibilities seem open. Either, we hold that Jesus, being the Divine Son of God, did actually multiply the loaves and the fishes. (Here we raise the theological question of what limitations in power were involved in the Incarnation. Is a true doctrine of it consistent with the possession of such power over nature?) Or, we may say that the whole story is historical except the statement that the people were 'filled' and there was food left over, and go on to explain it as a great open-air sacrament—a Galilean Lord's Supper—in which Jesus gave everyone a morsel of bread in token that those who had shared his table in obscurity would one day share it in his glory.[14]

The story of the raising of Lazarus poses two problems. First: Did Jesus really raise Lazarus from the dead? To this we may reply (1) that Jesus himself did claim to raise the dead (Luke 7.22; Matt. 11.5, Q) and that the synoptics record stories of two such raisings—the Widow of Nain's Son and Jairus' Daughter; and (2) that if Jesus is God Incarnate (as St John and most Christians believe) we cannot pronounce the raising incredible.

The other problem is the fact that the synoptics do not record the raising of Lazarus—an event which, in John's view, made the Jewish authorities resolve on Jesus' death (11.55). According to Mark 11.18 (though Barrett[15] rightly warns us not to rely too much on Mark's note), it was the Cleansing of the Temple—an event St John set early in the ministry—which provoked their fatal intervention. To this difficulty it may be replied that Mark's record of the Jerusalem ministry is demonstrably incomplete, and that Peter (whose witness, tradition says, lies behind Mark) may not have been present at the raising—he does not appear in John 7-12.

Moreover, John's story of the raising of Lazarus, however much it owes its present form to his own dramatic skill, not only contains many life-like touches—one thinks of the delineation of the characters of Martha and Mary and the 'agitation' of Jesus (11.33)—but makes the story of the Triumphal Entry as recorded by Mark coherent for the first time. Now we know why the people of Jerusalem treated Jesus' entry as a royal progress. The only evangelist who gives a sufficient reason for this is John who explicitly says that it was the report of the raising of Lazarus.

Perhaps no completely satisfactory explanation of this difficulty will ever be found. But we suggest that in view of the vivid circumstantiality of the narrative and of the abundant evidence that John had access to good and independent tradition about Jesus that the one thing we ought not to do is to dismiss this famous story as Johannine fiction.

NOTES

[1] C. H. Dodd, *H.T.F.G.*, p. 198; J. H. Bernard, *St John* I, p. clxxix.

[2] *The Evidences of Christianity* (1794).

[3] *Sēmeion* occurs 17 times in John. Five times Jesus' miracles are designated 'signs': Cana (2.11), the Officer's Son (4.54), the Feeding (6.14), the Man born Blind (9.16), the raising of Lazarus (12.18). The cure of the Bethesda Cripple is not specifically so called.

[4] See T. F. Glasson, *Moses in the Fourth Gospel* (1963).

[5] See R. Brown, *New Testament Essays*, pp. 185f. He rightly says that both the fourth gospel's words for miracle illustrate the OT concept of the God who acts. 'Work' stresses more the divine perspective of what is done (cf. 14·10, 'The Father who dwells in me does his works'). 'Sign' rather expresses the human psychological viewpoint, and so is a fitting term for others to apply to the miracles of Jesus.

[6] See H. W. Robinson's discussion in *Old Testament Essays*, pp. 1-17.

[7] R. H. Fuller, *Interpreting the Miracles*, p. 97. In the New Testament 'glory' (*doxa*) is an eschatological concept closely associated with 'kingdom' (*basileia*) and 'power' (*dynamis*)—as in the doxology to the Lord's Prayer, which is however later. If St John sees the whole incarnate life of Christ as a revelation of God's glory, he also regards it as climaxing in the Passion (13.31, 17.1), so that it may be said that for him the Cross is the glory *par excellence*—the supreme unveiling of God's presence in saving action.

[8] C. E. B. Cranfield, *S.J.T.*, March 1950, p. 60.

[9] To be precise, 98 times.

[10] See Alan Richardson, *History, Sacred and Profane* (1964).

[11] Cf. J. N. Sanders, *N.T.S.*, Sept. 1954, p. 30.

[12] See D. Guthrie in *Vox Evangelica* (1967), p. 81.

[13] *Jesus and the Word*, p. 173.

[14] C. H. Dodd (*H.T.F.G.*, p. 20) says Mark presents it not as a miracle but as a *mystery* story—'They did not understand about the loaves' (Mark 6.52).

[15] *The Gospel according to St John*, p. 323.

8

The Parables of St John's Gospel

'H o w is it,' asked Renan[1] in 1863, 'that the Gospel of John contains not one parable?' Since Renan countless critics[2] have repeated the statement, while allowing the presence of two allegories in the gospel (the Good Shepherd and the True Vine). Yet the statement is false.

What is a parable? *Mashal*, the Hebrew word for parable, is a very wide label for many kinds of figurative speech. So also is *parabolē* in the synoptic gospels: the word can cover everything from a simple metaphor to an elaborate story-parable. 'Physician, heal thyself' (Luke 4.23) is a parable, though it contains only three words; but so also is the Prodigal Son, which contains nearly four hundred. Mere length is no criterion; parables can be short as well as long; and parables are parables whether the evangelist has labelled them so or not. Once this is realized, we can go back to the Gospel of John, and find about a dozen passages which on the score of form, realism, and content, have as much right to be reckoned parables as the sixty or so parables in the synoptics.

We propose to isolate these Johannine parables and to comment on their authenticity and meaning.

I

1. *The Bridegroom and the Best Man* (John 3.29)

He who has the bride is the bridegroom; the friend of the bridegroom, who stands and hears him, rejoices greatly at the bridegroom's voice; therefore this joy of mine is now fulfilled (RSV).

The bridegroom's friend corresponds to the Hebrew *shoshbin*, our 'best man', whose part was to arrange the marriage contract, take part in the ceremony and preside at the wedding feast.

Here, on the Baptist's lips, we have a little parable, drawn, as a good parable should be, from real life. At a wedding, the chief person is not 'the best man' but the bridegroom. 'The best man' cheerfully plays second fiddle to him, and rejoices to attend and assist him. (For the metaphor of the 'bridegroom' on Jesus' lips see Mark 2.19f.) Even so, the Baptist, important as his role has been, gladly gives way to his great Successor.

Occurring as it does in a passage full of 'traditional' elements, this parable has every claim to go back to the Baptist himself. We know from the synoptics that the Baptist had a gift for vivid metaphor. And this passage can be shown[3] to contain evidences of Aramaic poetry exhibiting strophic arrangement and assonance.

2. *The Night Wind* (John 3.8)

The wind blows where it wills, and you hear the sound of it, but you do not know whence it comes or whither it goes; so it is with everyone who is born of the Spirit (RSV).

In structure this miniature parable closely resembles the Marcan parable of the Seed growing secretly (Mark 4.27), as its dominant idea—the spontaneity and mystery of natural processes—is the same. To be sure, the evangelist adapts it for his own theological purpose, but there is no cogent reason why the parable should not go back to One who

> spoke of grass, and wind, and rain,
> And figtrees and fair weather.

As Jesus talked to Nicodemus, the night wind rustled around their place of meeting. Here, ready to hand, was a vivid and apt analogy. 'Listen to the wind, Nicodemus,'[4] Jesus said to him, 'it blows where it wills: where it comes from and where it goes is a mystery. Yet how real and powerful a thing it is! So is God's wind —the Spirit.' Hebrew *ruach* like Greek *pneuma* means both 'wind' and 'spirit'; and to the Hebrew mind, the wind, invisible yet powerful, represented in nature the action of God's Spirit.

This image of the Night Wind was surely never the creation of the community or the evangelist. Here we have a true Dominical *obiter dictum*, presumably remembered by the man to whom it was uttered—Nicodemus.

3. *The Harvest* (John 4.35-38)

Do you not say 'Four months more and then comes the harvest'? But look, I tell you, look round on the fields, they are already white, ripe for harvest. The reaper is drawing his pay and gathering a crop for *eternal life* so that sower and reaper may rejoice together. That is how the saying comes *true*: 'One sows and another reaps.' I sent you to reap a crop for which you have not toiled. Others toiled and you have come in for the harvest of their toil (NEB).

Here, in the story of Jesus' journey through Samaria, we have a parabolic saying which, despite some Johannine elements (see the words italicized) has a strong claim to be regarded as 'traditional'. Its agricultural imagery can be paralleled at many points from the synoptic parables, as its general theme—the presence of the Kingdom figured under the symbol of harvest—is echoed in the Q passage:

The harvest is plentiful, but the labourers are few. Pray therefore the Lord of the harvest to send out labourers into his harvest (Luke 10.2; Matt. 9.37f.).

There are no good grounds for supposing that John knew this little 'Q' parable and simply elaborated it to suit his purpose. Rather this parabolic saying must have come to the evangelist from his own independent source of tradition. On the other hand, there is ample confirmation in the synoptics for the point of 'realized eschatology' which it makes: the harvest is at hand; the reaper has overtaken the sower; it is the promised age of fulfilment.

4. *The Apprenticed Son* (John 5.19-20a)

Truly, truly I tell you, a son[5] can do nothing by himself; he only does what he sees his father doing; what the father does, the son does. For the father loves the son, and shows him all he himself is doing.

Here, embedded in a christological passage about the relation between Jesus and the Father, C. H. Dodd[6] has uncovered a brief parable which he names 'the Apprenticed Son'. Its realism is attested by contemporary legal contracts, found in Egyptian papyri, in which the apprentice is required to do all that his master does.

In the preceding verses in John's gospel Jesus has been charged with 'making himself equal to his Father'. Now, in rabbinical idiom, it was a *rebellious* son who was said to 'make himself equal to his father'. Jesus proceeds to deny the charge made by his Jewish critics: so far from being a rebel, the soul of his sonship is obedience. And the first point in his *apologia* is a little parable which, like that of the Splinter and the Plank (Matt. 7.3-5, Q), may very well reflect the youthful experience of 'the carpenter's son' (Matt. 13.34) in the shop at Nazareth.

Think (says Jesus) of a son apprenticed to his father's trade. (Such a family arrangement must have been common enough in the simple society of Palestine.) He does not hammer or chisel away on his own untutored impulse. Rather, he watches his father at work and copies every action. And, in turn, the affectionate father initiates his son into all the tricks of the trade.

Just so, says Jesus, I imitate my heavenly Father. I do what he does. And I tell you, incredulous Jews (here the parable ends and the application begins), that he will show me the secret of still greater works.

5. *Slave and Son* (John 8.35)

J. H. Bernard found it so hard to link up v. 35 with what precedes and what follows that he suggested it might be a gloss. (In the verses which precede the contrast is between the *free man* and the *slave*, but in v. 35 it changes suddenly to the gradation in a household between a *slave* and a *son*.) The true solution, however, is to see in the verse a tiny parable which had once an independent existence.

Since *eis ton aiōna* need mean no more than 'permanently' and the definite article before 'slave' and 'son' is probably generic, the meaning is: 'A slave does not stay permanently in the household, but a son does.' We may compare the father's word to the elder brother in Luke 15.31 'My boy, you are always with me.'

If this is a little parable of Jesus (as Dodd and Jeremias agree), to whom did he originally speak it and to what end? The synoptic parable most like to it is that of the Asking Son (Matt 7.9-11; Luke 11.11-13) in which Jesus bids his disciples trust God more. This one also was probably addressed to the disciples; but its point is rather their possession of the privilege of sonship and the assurance that they may rest secure in their heavenly Father's care. (Cf. Rom. 8.15 with its contrast between the spirit of slavery and the spirit of sonship which makes believers cry Abba, Father.)

6. *The Shepherd* (John 10.1-5)

In truth I tell you, in very truth, the man who does not enter the sheep-fold by the door, but climbs in some other way, is nothing but a thief or a robber. The man who enters by the door is the shepherd in charge of the sheep. The door-keeper admits him, and the sheep hear his voice;

he calls his own sheep by name, and leads them out. When he has
brought them all out, he goes ahead, and the sheep follow, because they
know his voice. They will not follow a stranger; they will run away
from him, because they do not recognize the voice of strangers (NEB).

This is 'a simple parable drawn from early Palestinian tradition'.[7]
Its pastoral imagery recalls the 'shepherd' sayings in the synoptics
(Mark 6.34, 14.27; Matt. 10.16; Luke 15.3-6, 19.10), and Jesus'
description of the disciples as his 'little flock' (Luke 12.32; cf. Mic.
5.4). For Old Testament background, we remember that in Ezek. 34
(cf. also 37.24) God denounces the false shepherds (or rulers) of
Israel and promises to set over his people a Shepherd Messiah of
David's line. These are our main clues to the thrust and meaning
of the Johannine parable.

The sheepfold signifies Israel, as the parable is directed against
Jesus' Jewish opponents (9.34, 10.6, 19). Right through John 10 and
specially clear in vv. 24-26 ('If you are the Messiah tell us plainly'),
runs the question of Jesus' Messianic authority. It is this challenge
to his authority that provides the historical setting for the parable
which not only answers his critics but makes a veiled Messianic
claim. 'I am no interloper but the rightful Shepherd,' Jesus says in
effect; 'I need no signs to prove my authority which is self-
authenticating; it lies in the fact that my sheep follow my leader-
ship because they recognize in me the accents and actions of the
true Shepherd of God's flock, while they refuse to follow false
shepherds.'

'This was a parable that Jesus told them,' comments the evangelist (10.6). 'They' are the rulers of Israel in Jesus' day, and the
parable is yet another 'weapon of war' in his controversy with
them. What follows in John 10.7ff. is a typical Eastern paraphrase
of the two ideas of the parable with reference to Christ.

7. The Benighted Traveller (John 11.9f.)

Are there not twelve hours of daylight? If anyone walks in the daytime
he does not stumble because he sees the light of the world. But if he
walks at night he stumbles, because the light fails him (NEB).

With its opening rhetorical question and its two antithetical
conditional clauses, this has all the style of a parable. It shows few
Johannine marks. And, as a parable should, it deals in matter of
familiar, everyday experience—the difference between walking
in daylight and walking in unlit darkness. (Incidentally, for us the
contrast between light and darkness suggests the contrast between

knowledge and ignorance. For the Hebrew it is primarily the difference between security and danger.)

As we have it now, the parable is part of the Lazarus story, i.e. it belongs to that stage in Jesus' ministry when events were moving to their inexorable climax and his life began to be in real danger (11.8, 53). Though the geography is different, and the time earlier, we may compare Luke 13.31-33 when the Pharisees brought Jesus word of Herod's murderous designs. Probably John's setting for the parable is basically right: it is a Crisis parable—one of many (the Defendant, the Rich Fool, the Burglar, etc.), in which Jesus sought to alert his hearers to the gravity of the impending catastrophe. 'You,' he said to them, 'are in the plight and peril of the benighted traveller. You must act before daylight goes and the dark comes.'

8. *The Journeyer at Sunset* (John 12.35f.)

The light is among you still, but not for long. Go on your way while you have the light, so that the darkness may not overtake you. He who journeys in the dark does not know where he is going. While you have the light, trust to the light, that you may become sons of light (NEB).

We take this parable next, because it sounds like a companion to the Benighted Traveller.

Again we have a comparison from real life, turning on the difference between walking in the light and walking in the dark, with an injunction to 'step it out' (as we say) 'while the going is good'. It is another parable of Crisis, as indeed the preceding verses show, 'Now is the hour of judgment for this world; now shall the Prince of this world be driven out' (12.31, NEB). The reference is to the 'lifting up' of the Son of man and the judgment it will bring in its train. John's historical setting for the parable seems right. In it Jesus says to those around him, 'The darkness of judgment is approaching. You have still time, but not much, to make your decision, and escape the impending doom.'

9. *The Grain of Wheat* (John 12.24)

Truly, truly, I say to you, unless a grain of wheat falls into the ground and dies, it remains alone; but if it dies, it bears much fruit (RSV).

On the score of imagery, form and vocabulary, this has strong claims to rank as a genuine parable of Jesus.

The conditional clauses, showing antithetic parallelism, resemble those in the parable of the Single Eye (Matt. 6.22f.; Luke 11.34).

Semitic influence appears in the generic definite article ('the grain').
The synoptic tradition has a parable about a grain of (mustard)
seed which after sowing 'in the ground', grew into a great plant in
whose branches 'the birds of the air' came to roost.[8] Finally, our
parable is immediately followed by a saying of Jesus which, in
spite of Johannine colouring, has synoptic equivalents (12.25).

What was the parable's original meaning? Some have interpreted
generally, on the lines of 'there is no gain except by loss, there
is no life except by death'. This is very unlikely. In the gospel the
parable is set in the penumbra of the Passion, and N. A. Dahl[9] is
surely right in referring it to the eschatological fulfilment wrought
by the death of the grain of wheat. Like the synoptic saying about
'the ransom' (Mark 10.45), it has to do with the necessity and
purpose of his Passion. Jesus is thinking of his own death and the
great fulfilment it will bring with it.

Now the synoptic tradition has preserved another vivid metaphor—or rather mixture of metaphors—which helps us to understand how he thought of it:

> I have come to set fire to the earth, and how I wish it were already
> kindled! I have a baptism to undergo, and how hampered I am until the
> ordeal is over (Luke 12.49f., NEB).

Before the fire can blaze, Jesus says, I must die. (He is the new
Prometheus and must pay the same price.) But he says more. His
baptism in blood, he suggests, is a kind of emancipation, an
initiation into fuller and freer activity. This is in substance what
The Grain of Wheat says also: the death of Jesus is the ineluctable
precondition of his ministry becoming greatly fruitful for 'the
many'.

Scholars have noted how close is the resemblance between the
parable and Paul's words in I Cor. 15.36: 'The seed that you sow
does not come to life unless it has first died.' If Paul knew the
Lord's parable about the Thief, as I Thess. 5.2ff. implies, it is very
possible that he knew this one about the Grain of Wheat.

10. *The Woman in Labour* (John 16.21)

> A woman in labour is in pain because her time has come; but when
> the child is born she forgets the anguish in her joy that a man has been
> born into the world (NEB).

This parable comes from the Farewell Discourses where Jesus
applies it to his disciples thus:

So it is with you : for the moment you are sad at heart; but I shall see you again, and then you will be joyful, and no one shall rob you of your joy.

In structure our parable resembles Luke's version of the Strong Man Armed (Luke 11.21f.) and, partly, Mark's Seed Growing Secretly (Mark 4.26-29). It draws on very familiar human experience, and it shows little sign of Johannine 'discoloration'. (Professor Dodd,[10] indeed, finds traces of John's own style in the phrases 'into the world' and 'her time'. Yet it is not necessarily so. 'One who comes into the world' was a rabbinical phrase for a human being. 'Her time' may well echo Isa. 26.17 'Like a woman with child . . . when she is near her time.'[11] In any case it is the natural and universal way of describing the beginning of a woman's labour pains.)

Some commentators have made the parable teach the general truth that pain is often the necessary precursor of joy. More recent ones have rightly seen that this parable has an Old Testament background and is in fact an image of Messianic suffering and triumph. Thus in Isa. 26.17ff., which is a prayer for God's vindication of his people, Israel is compared to a pregnant woman who 'cries out in pain when she is near her time'. There follows—and it is the first clear hint of the doctrine in the Old Testament—the promise of resurrection : 'The dead shall live, their bodies shall rise'; and 'the dwellers in the dust' are bidden to 'sing for joy'. Equally important is Isa. 66.7-14. In this eschatological passage Jerusalem's suffering is likened to a woman 'in labour and pain', till there comes to her a deliverance like the joy of successful childbirth. And the passage ends with words closely resembling John 16.22 : 'You shall see and your heart shall rejoice.'

Thus the parable in John is shot through with resurrection imagery. Hoskyns[12] thought it might well preserve 'the true originals of the belief of the primitive Church and of the Lord himself that Christ must suffer death and rise again according to the scriptures'.

II

We have isolated ten Johannine parables. Can we unearth any more? There are three 'possibles' : the Father's House, the True Vine and the Footwashing.

11. *The Father's House* (John 14.2f.)

> In my Father's house are many rooms. If it were not so, I would have
> told you, for I go to prepare a place for you; and if I go and prepare a
> place for you, I will come again and receive you to myself, that where
> I am you may be also (RSV).

Burney[13] finds in these verses the four-beat rhythm which we
find in Matthew's version of the Lord's Prayer and elsewhere, as
well as an example of step-parallelism, also characteristic of Jesus'
teaching. These are for him marks of authenticity. But the really
interesting point is the correspondence between John 14.1-6 and
the synoptic account of the preparation for the Last Supper.
According to Mark 14.12-16, two disciples *went forth to prepare*
a guest room where Jesus and his disciples might meet. They *did
not know the way*, and were bidden to follow a man who would
lead them to the house and its owner. In the event they found a
large upper room *prepared*, as Jesus *had told* them.

Against this background the words of John 14.1ff. become readily
intelligible. The suggestion is that Jesus turned the disciples' errand
of the previous day (was the story familiar in John's circle?) into
a parable of eternity and made the Upper Room foreshadow the
heavenly home of God. It is an attractive suggestion.

12. *The True Vine* (John 15.1f.)

> I am the true vine, and my Father is the gardener. Every barren branch
> of mine he cuts away, and every fruiting branch he cleans to make it
> more fruitful still (NEB).

For centuries ordinary Christians have believed these to be
words of Jesus. Have they been mistaken?

We do not settle the question negatively merely by murmuring
the word 'allegory'. Despite Jülicher, some of Jesus' parables have
strong allegorical elements, as rabbinical parables often had. Once
this prejudice is out of the way, we can look at John 15.1f. with
fresh eyes.

No one disputes that the 'viticulture' of the parable is true to
life. In some ways the parable resembles the Lucan parable of the
Barren Figtree (Luke 13.6-9) which was planted in a vineyard.

The phrase 'the true vine' clearly echoes Jer. 2.21. For centuries
the vine had been a symbol for Israel, the people of God; and in
an allegorical parable (Mark 12.1-9) based on Isa. 5.1-7, which
speaks of a good vine gone bad, Jesus had warned the Israel of the

day of God's impending judgment, prophesying that God would give the vineyard to others.

If Jesus knew himself as the Son of man called to embody in himself the destiny of the new Israel[14]—and in Ps. 80.17 the vine of God, Israel, is actually called 'the son of man'—if he knew that one of his 'branches' was even then defecting, might he not well have applied to himself Jeremiah's words about 'the true vine', and used them for warning and encouragement—more especially as, on that evening, he made 'the fruit of the vine' the effective symbol of the New Covenant he was about to establish with his blood?

13. *The Footwashing* (John 13.1-15)

Jesus did not confine himself to *spoken* parable: like the Old Testament prophet he often preferred to teach by an *ōth*—a symbolic deed, a parabolic action charged with Messianic significance. Thus he rode into Jerusalem on an ass; he cleansed the Temple; and in the Upper Room he enacted a great double parable with bread and wine.

To this same class of actions belongs the Footwashing. Though none of the synoptics records it—unless a fragmentary echo of it survives in Luke 22.37, 'I am among you as one who serves'—its essential historicity is to be affirmed.[15] To be sure, the theological hand of the evangelist is to be discerned in vv. 1-3 and 11; but I can find no good reason for questioning the actual event, the tale of Peter's protest, or the words of Jesus urging his disciples to copy the love that stooped to serve.

How is the passage to be interpreted? Recall first that the whole episode is enacted in the shadow of the Cross, and that the Washer of the disciples' feet is the One who 'takes away the sin of the world'. Notice, next, the verbs used to describe his actions. Jesus 'lays aside' (*tithēsin*) his garments and, the washing completed, 'takes them' (*elaben*) again. These are the very verbs[16] which the Good Shepherd had used of his death and resurrection (10.11, 15, 17f.). Above all, remember that the motif of the whole narrative is cleansing, and that Jesus said to Peter, 'If I do not wash you, you are not in fellowship with me.' The meaning, then, is that there is no room in Jesus' fellowship for those who refuse to be cleansed by his atoning death. The later summons to humble service is the corollary of what Jesus does for his disciples. Because they have been redeemed by the death of the Servant Son of God, they must show their gratitude in the service of others. *Noblesse oblige*.

On this interpretation, the Footwashing is, like the double parable of the bread and the wine, an acted parable foreshadowing the Cross and giving the disciples (in Otto's phrase) 'a share in the power of the broken Christ'.

III

If our arguments are sound, the statement that the fourth gospel has no parables badly needs revision. There are in fact about a dozen. Some, it is true, are very short, and none is comparable in length with the story-parables of the synoptics. Yet, brief as they are, they shed light on the mission and message of him who told them.

Early church fathers like Tertullian and Origen tended to find Christ everywhere in the parables, so that their allegorical ingenuities excite the scornful smiles of the modern scholar. But were their exegetical instincts so misguided?

As the Beatitudes contain veiled Messianic claims, so do the parables of Jesus in the synoptic gospels. True, neither in Beatitudes nor parables does Jesus call himself Messiah (this of course consists with 'the Messianic Secret'); none the less in both the implication is that Jesus, by speaking and acting as he does, is speaking and acting as God's representative or vice-gerent—as his Messiah.

'Jesus hides himself behind the parables,' Ernst Fuchs[17] has said, 'they are veiled self-testimony, and Jesus is the secret content.' What Fuchs finds true of the synoptic parables is no less true of the parables in the fourth gospel. The parable of the Shepherd carries a veiled Messianic claim. So, much more explicitly because he is talking to his own disciples in the privacy of the Upper Room, does the True Vine. The Apprenticed Son testifies to Jesus' sense of unique Sonhood. The Benighted Traveller and the Journeyer at Sunset are parables of Crisis—that supreme crisis in God's dealings with his people in which Jesus is the central figure. Likewise, the Grain of Wheat and the Woman in Labour speak, in their different ways, of eschatological fulfilment, of the Messiah's triumph through suffering and death and the rich harvest it will bring.

The parables in the fourth gospel, therefore, illuminate both our Lord's conception of his person and the purpose of his dying. Were the early fathers so fantastically wrong after all? By our canons of scientific exegesis they stand convicted of allegorizing *ad absurdum.* But if Jesus is indeed 'the secret content' of the parables, if they contain 'veiled self-testimony', if through them glimmers 'the veiled kingliness' of the Saviour, their 'absurdity' is not so wide of the truth.

NOTES

[1] *The Life of Jesus*, p. 12.

[2] See G. H. C. Macgregor, *The Gospel of John*, p. xvii.

[3] M. Black, *An Aramaic Approach*, p. 147.

[4] I recall a memorable sermon of J. S. Stewart whose refrain was 'Listen to the wind, Nicodemus'. See now his book, *The Wind of the Spirit*.

[5] Lit. 'the son'. The Semite uses the definite article where we should use the indefinite one. Cf. 'the grain of wheat' in 12.24.

[6] *H.T.F.G.*, p. 386. See also his article in *Revue d'histoire et de philosophie religieuse*, 42, (1962), pp. 107-115.

[7] J. Jeremias, *T.W.N.T.*, vi, p. 494. Dr. J. A. T. Robinson (*Twelve New Testament Studies*, pp. 67-75) finds in John 10.1-5 the fusion of two parables. I do not find his case for evidence of 'suture' convincing and prefer to maintain the parable's unity. Note that John's word for parable *paroimia* is not different in meaning from the synoptic *parabolē*: they are variant translations of the Hebrew *mashal*.

[8] The phrase 'much fruit' (John 12.24) occurs in the LXX version of Dan. 3.12 which is echoed in Mark 4.32.

[9] *Studia Theologica*, 5 (1951), p. 155.

[10] *H.T.F.G.*, p. 371.

[11] The phrase 'a little while' (Isa. 26.20) occurs seven times in John 16.16-19.

[12] *The Fourth Gospel*, p. 488.

[13] *The Poetry of our Lord*, pp. 93, 126ff.

[14] 'In the end it is Jesus himself who appears as the single bearer of Israel's destiny. If the nation will not bear the burden, then it must be borne alone. . . . On the Cross he is in very truth Israel, Israel as God determined it. . . . The old Israel dies in him, but in the very same instant the new Israel is born.' (C. W. F. Smith, *The Jesus of the Parables*, pp. 287f.)

[15] See J. A. T. Robinson, *Neotestamentica et Patristica* (1966), pp. 144-7.

[16] *Tithenai tēn psychēn* is a Semitism. 'Give one's life' (Mark 10.45) and 'lay down one's life' are variant translations of *sith napshō* in Isa. 53.10.

[17] *T.L.Z.*, 79, (1954), col. 345-8. See also the last chapter of C. W. F. Smith's fine book *The Jesus of the Parables* (1946). The parables as well as the Cross, he says, present us with the problem of the Person of Christ. In them Jesus appears not as a sage or as a moralist but 'as the Initiator of God's new age and the Agent of his purpose'. Whether he explicitly claimed to be the Messiah or not, 'he said those things which none short of the Messiah had the authority to say'.

9

The Sayings of Jesus in St John

'I F Jesus spoke as Matthew represents,' said Renan[1] a hundred years ago, 'he cannot have spoken as John relates.' In the succeeding century many others have reached the same conclusion. True, or false?

The question is important—more important, *pace* the philosophers, than the question whether the dialogues of Plato preserve the words and ideas of Socrates. For centuries John's gospel has been 'the text-book of the parish priest and the inspiration of the straightforward layman'.[2] They have used its words as words of Jesus to comfort both in life and death. But what if the sayings of Jesus in John are not in any sense words of Jesus?

That there is a sharp difference between, say, the Sermon on the Mount in Matthew and the subtle arguments of Jesus in John 5, 8 and 10 or the sacred farewells of John 14-16, is not to be disputed. Must we therefore conclude that St John has succeeded in passing off on the Church his own thoughts and fancies, or those of his fellow Christians, in the guise of actual words of the Lord?

I

We have seen that the statement that John's gospel contains no parables (whereas there are at least sixty in the synoptics) is not true. But if we here confine ourselves to non-parabolic sayings, we may begin by noting, with C. F. Burney,[3] that, whatever be their theological content, the sayings of Jesus in St John are often couched in the same forms of semitic poetry as we find on Jesus' lips in the synoptics. Thus *synonymous* parallelism appears in

He who comes to me shall not hunger,
And he who believes in me shall never thirst (6.35).

antithetic parallelism in

For judgment I came into this world,
That they who do not see may see,
And those who see may become blind (9.39)

and *step* parallelism in

I go to prepare a place for you,
And if I go and prepare a place for you
I will come again and will take you to myself (14.2f.).

We even find in John a parallel couplet followed by a clinching comment—cf. John 4.36 with Mark 2.27.

These examples are only a tithe of Burney's evidence that the Johannine sayings of Jesus are often clothed in the same poetic forms as the teaching of Jesus in the synoptics. Their poetic form does not automatically prove them words of the Lord. We may, if we will, credit the poetic form of the sayings to the fourth evangelist. The trouble about this suggestion is that we do not know that the evangelist had this poetic gift. We do know, from the synoptic gospels, that Jesus had.

Thus Burney's work does go some way to authenticate the Johannine sayings of Jesus.

II

Next, careful search will uncover in the fourth gospel more than two dozen synoptic-like sayings of Jesus. These logia, though verbally different, are so alike in purport to their synoptic counterparts that they look like variants in a common oral tradition. Here are some examples:

2.19 'Destroy this temple and in three days I will raise it up.' (Cf. Mark 14.58; Acts 6.14.)

6.51 'The bread which I will give for the life of the world is my flesh.' (Cf. Luke 22.19; I Cor. 11.24.) This is the Johannine version of Jesus' 'word' over the bread.

12.25 'He who loves his life loses it, and he who hates his life in this world will keep it for eternal life.' (Cf. Matt. 10.39; Mark 8.35; Luke 9.24.)

13.16 'A servant is not greater than his master, nor is he who is sent greater than he who sent him.' (Cf. Matt. 10.24; Luke 6.40.)

13.20 'He who receives any one whom I send receives me, and he who receives me receives him who sent me.' (Cf. Matt. 10.40; Mark 9.37; Luke 10.16.)

16.23 'If you ask anything of the Father, he will give it you in my name . . . ask, and you will receive.' (Cf. Matt. 7.7; Luke 11.9; Matt. 21.22.)

18.11 'Put your sword in its sheath; shall I not drink the cup which the Father has given me?' (Cf. Matt. 26.52; Mark 10.39, 14.36.)

20.23 'If you forgive the sins of any, they are forgiven; if you retain the sins of any, they are retained.' (Cf. Matt. 18.18.)

To these we may add the three *hypsoun*[4] sayings:

3.14 'As Moses lifted up the serpent in the wilderness, so *must the Son of man* be lifted up.'

8.28 'When you have lifted up *the Son of man*, then you will know that I am he.'

12.32ff. 'And I, when I am lifted up from the earth, will draw all men to myself. . . . How can you say that *the Son of man must* be lifted up?'

These correspond to the three synoptic predictions of the Passion (Mark 8.31, 9.31, 10.32f.). They seem to echo Isa. 52.13 ('My servant . . . shall be *lifted up*'); and since they are less detailed than their synoptic equivalents, are conceivably more ancient than they.

There must be many more Dominical sayings embedded in John's gospel which we cannot include in our list because we lack authenticating synoptic parallels. Here are some logia from the fourth gospel which, if we cannot precisely parallel them, have undoubtedly a synoptic ring about them:

4.34 'My food is to do the will of him that sent me and to accomplish his work.'

4.48 'Unless you see signs and wonders, you will not believe.'

12.31 'Now is the judgment of this world, now shall the ruler of this world be cast out.'

14.2 'In my Father's house are many rooms.'

18.36 'My kingship is not of this world.'

He would be a very sceptical critic who would categorically assert that Jesus could not have uttered 'short and concise' sayings like these.

III

From synoptic-like sayings we move on to synoptic-like dialogues in John.

The oral tradition behind the synoptics preserved a number of dialogues between Jesus and his disciples or his critics. Their general pattern was a note of the occasion, an interchange of speech between the two parties, and then the Lord's pronouncement on the matter.

But if we imagine that this kind of dialogue is confined to the synoptics, we are mistaken: by a wise use of Form Criticism C. H. Dodd[5] has laid bare half a dozen such dialogues in the fourth gospel.

3.25-30 *The Baptist's Disclaimer.* The occasion is a discussion about 'purifying'. There follows a dialectical exchange between the Baptist and his disciples. And the dialogue ends with the Baptist's parable about the Bridegroom and the Best Man.

4.31-34 *The Food of Jesus.* In form this resembles Mark 3.31-35; in content Matt. 4.1-4.

6.66-70 *Peter's Confession.* Compare the dialogue at Caesarea Philippi (Mark 8.27-30).

7.3-8 *Jesus and his Brothers.* In form and content this resembles the dialogue between the Pharisees and Jesus in Luke 13.31-33, which is also associated with his departure from Galilee.

9.2-5 *Who sinned?* This conversation is very like the 'theodicy' dialogue in Luke 13.1-5.

9.39-41 *The Blindness of the Pharisees.* With Jesus' 'For judgment I came' compare Luke 12.49, with the Pharisees' protest ('are we also blind?') the lawyer's protest in Luke 11.45, and with Jesus' charge of blindness his saying in the synoptics about the blind leading the blind (Matt. 15.14; Luke 6. 39).

That these six dialogues contain 'Johannisms' and have been used for his own purposes is clear. It is equally clear that in them he is not inventing but reaching back into the common oral tradition about Jesus.

IV

But there are other criteria of authenticity which we may apply—Schmiedel's, for example.

Schmiedel, it will be remembered, in arguing with the 'Christ myth' school, picked out nine synoptic sayings[6] which he said must be genuine because they could not have been invented by the early Church.

If we apply a like test to the fourth gospel, certain Johannine sayings of Jesus appear equally 'uninventable'.

One is John 5.17: 'My Father is working still, and I am working.'

This, St John tells us, was Jesus' reply to those who criticized him
for healing on the sabbath. Clearly it contradicts Genesis 2.3; and
we may fairly claim that this bold criticism of Holy Writ was
never invented by the early Christians. The saying means that 'the
laws of Nature and of Right and Wrong do not observe the sabbath. The same Father whom Jesus saw making his sun shine on
the evil and on the good, made his sun shine on the sabbath and
on the week-day.'[7]

Another such passage is John 10.33-36.

Mark 12.35-37 is synoptic evidence that Jesus, teaching in the
Temple precincts, could refute his Jewish critics from the letter of
scripture—in this case Ps. 110.1. In John 10.33-36, Jesus, again in
the Temple precincts, directs his opponents to Ps. 82.6 ('I say, you
are gods, sons of the Most High, all of you'). His argument is an
a fortiori one: 'If scripture, whose authority you will not question,
calls men (in this case, judges) commissioned by God to act for
him "gods", One whom the Father has made his consecrated am-
bassador to the world can hardly be accused of blasphemy for
calling himself "God's son". If human leaders can be called "gods",
how much more may One greater than they make a lesser claim
—to be not God but God's son.'

The argument implies a kind of belief in the divinity of man in
relation to God's purposes. Such an argument, which does not
clearly set Jesus apart from other men, would hardly have been
invented by the early Church.

Both these examples come from accounts of Jesus' controversy
with Jerusalem Jews. It is in fact these controversial discourses
(especially John, chapter 8) which have seemed to many Christian
scholars to have the least claim to authenticity because they apparently reflect the later debate between the Church and the
synagogue. Jewish scholars, interestingly enough, have taken an
opposite view, arguing as Israel Abrahams[8] did, that John's gospel
'enshrines a genuine tradition of an aspect of Jesus' teaching which
has not found a place in the synoptics'.

This judgment is worth serious pondering. The point is that, for
the most part, in such Johannine discourses Jesus is addressing
a quite different audience from that presupposed in the synoptics.
There his hearers are Galilean peasants; in John 7-10 they are Jerusalem rabbis or their like. And it may fairly be urged that you do
not use the same method of argument in debating with scholastics

as in talking to simple country folk. On the contrary, you try to meet your critics on their own ground and beat them with their own weapons. Now, for the Jerusalem scribes, 'theology' meant largely the exegesis and application of Old Testament texts, and it is surely no accident that our two examples were of this sort, involving as they did Gen. 2.3 and Ps. 82.6.[9] This principle, that a different audience requires a different mode of argument, may well dispose us to look again at Jesus' polemics in chapters 7 and 8 and ask ourselves whether we are not often in fact dealing with words of Jesus and not merely echoes of the later debate between the Church and the synagogue.

V

We may make yet another—quite different approach—to this problem of authenticity. Browning[10] once wrote of 'points' in the gospel tradition which had become 'stars' in St John's perception of them. E. A. Abbott[11] considered the correct analogy was that of 'inspired targums', i.e. free paraphrases of authentic words of Jesus. And Johannes Weiss[12] liked to think of 'grains of gold from Jesus' sayings' which St John has beaten out in the discourses of the fourth gospel. All three were thinking of the same thing—the elaboration, or expansion, in John of something essentially historical, something that goes back to Jesus himself.

Jesus' use of *'Father' as a name for God* is a good example. This is not so common in the synoptics as many suppose. The figures for the four gospel sources are as follows: Mark:4, Q:8, Luke:6 and Matt: about 20. The count in St John is 107, so that it has truly been said that it is John primarily among the evangelists who has made 'Father' the natural name for God among Christians.

Why is it that in the synoptics the Fatherhood of God is something of which Jesus speaks quite rarely, and mostly to his disciples? It is precisely because the experience of Abba, Father, was the supreme reality of his own life, an experience of unparalleled intensity and depth. (From this unique experience sprang his authority—his complete dependence on the Father was the source of his astonishing independence of men—a point made times without number in the fourth gospel.) When therefore St John represents Jesus as calling God Father more than a hundred times, he is not importing something alien into the mind and message of Jesus; he is bringing out something which was absolutely basic to it.

So, too, with our Lord's *sense of unique sonship*. Twice in the synoptic gospels (Mark 12.6f. and 13.32) Jesus refers to himself as God's son; and in a third passage he claims not only that he is the organ of God's self-revelation but that he alone knows God truly as Father and for that supreme knowledge all men must become debtors to him (Matt. 11.27; Luke 10.22). Now observe how these 'grains of gold' are beaten out in St John's gospel:

'The Father loves the Son and has given all things into his hand' (3.38).

'All that my Father has is mine' (16.15).

'The Father knows me and I know the Father' (10.15).

'No one comes to the Father but by me' (14.6).

Cf. also the parable of the Apprenticed Son (5.19f.).

A third example is Jesus' promise of *the helping Spirit*. The synoptics preserve three or four sayings in which Jesus promises his disciples that in future time of trial they may count on the power and guidance of the Spirit. 'Say whatever is given you in that hour, for it is not you who speak, but the Holy Spirit' (Mark 13.11). 'The Holy Spirit will teach you in that very hour what you ought to say' (Luke 12.12; Matt. 10.20). 'Behold, I send the promise of my Father upon you' (Luke 24.28). So also the early Christians cherished as a word of Jesus the declaration, 'You shall receive power when the Holy Spirit has come upon you' (Acts 1.8).

It may fairly be claimed that the five sayings about the Paraclete ('Helper', 'Advocate') in John 14-16 simply spell out in fuller and richer Johannine terms the teaching of Jesus about the helping Spirit found in the synoptics. Inspired airs based on original themes, they form an essential part of our Lord's teaching concerning the Holy Spirit.[13]

VI

Sayings of Jesus in John cast in the poetic forms we know he employed, logia echoing similar ones in the first three gospels, dialogues clearly 'traditional' in form and content, passages evidently beyond the invention of the early Church, sayings which are inspired paraphrases of 'nuclear' words of Jesus—these have formed the staple of our study. It is time now to consider the authenticity of the discourses as wholes.

Suppose we first consider the Discourse on the Bread of Life (6.25-50).[14] Is this a Johannine construction in which the evangelist, seeking to declare the true meaning of something important in the gospel tradition, portrays Jesus as 'the answer to the desire of men for food and a king'.[15] Or does it have a claim, despite its Johannine colouring, to represent what Jesus said, near Passover time, in the Capernaum synagogue (6.4, 59)?

Much more can be said for the second view than our critical scholars have for long allowed.

First: it can be shown—see our chapter on the gospel tradition —that the historical setting of the Discourse rests back on early and reliable tradition. This, so far as it goes, creates an initial presumption in its favour.

Second: Peder Borgen[16] has shown that the Discourse reproduces the pattern of Jewish synagogue preaching. The preacher first took a text, generally from the Pentateuch, which he then paraphrased. His ensuing homily commented on the text almost word for word. Commonly within the homily came a subordinate citation from the prophets, with a few lines of commentary developing the main one. Finally the statement that opened the homily was repeated, or recalled, at the end.

Now in John 6.31-50 we find this pattern. 6.31 has the text from the Pentateuch (Ex. 16.4, 15; cf. Ps. 78.24). In vv. 32f. Jesus paraphrases and corrects it in typically Jewish fashion ('Do not read . . . but . . .'). Vv. 35-50 form the main homily in which Jesus comments in turn on 'bread', 'from heaven' and 'eating'. The subordinate citation from the prophets (Isa. 54.13) comes in v. 45. Finally in v. 48 he repeats v. 35—indeed in vv. 49f. even the text and its paraphrase are taken up again.

Third: The work of Aileen Guilding[17] and others on the Jewish lectionary has shown that the Old Testament readings in synagogue around Passover time included the narratives of the manna (Ex. 16; Num. 11), Isa. 54-55, and the story of the Tree of Life (Gen. 3). Now the theme of John 6.25-50 is the new manna from heaven, and practically all these Old Testament passages are quoted or echoed in it.

Corroboration of this third point may be sought in B. Gärtner's argument[18] that the Discourse reflects, both in form and content, the Jewish Passover *Haggadah*. (For example, we find in it the 'tripartite construction'—(1) significant event, (2) questioning and (3) interpretation—characteristic of the Passover *Haggadah*. We also find presupposed the doctrine of the three breads—the Wilderness manna, the Passover bread, and the bread of the world to come, the Messianic bread—which underlay the theology of the *Haggadah*.)

At this point we may recall that, according to Luke 4.17ff., Jesus did once before, in the Nazareth synagogue, take what *may* have been the *haphtarah* for the day (Isa. 61) and use it to proclaim that the Messianic prophecies were fulfilled in his mission and message. Why should he not, later in his ministry, have proclaimed himself, in sapiential terms,[19] the fulfilment of the promised bread from heaven? In short, John 6.25-50, for all its Johannine style, may well preserve the substance of what Jesus said as 'he was teaching in synagogue in Capernaum'.

Consider next Jesus' words at the feast of Dedication (10.22-40). The impression made by a first reading of the passage is that we have here a typical piece of Johannine theologizing with no title to be the record of an actual controversy between Jesus and the Jerusalem authorities. 'You do not believe because you are not of my sheep', 'I and the Father are one', 'Believe the works, that you may know and understand that the Father is in me, and I in the Father'—could anything be more unmistakably Johannine?

But, as a little philosophy inclines man's mind to atheism, whereas depth in it inclines his heart to religion, so a closer study of the passage in John suggests other conclusions.

We have already quoted Scott Holland's comment on vv. 22f. This note of time and place so rings with authenticity that even Bultmann calls it 'a piece of tradition'. But we may, in passing, underscore one detail of accurate topography. In the winter when the cold winds sweep in from the wilderness Jesus is found in the eastern colonnade (known as Solomon's), the only one whose closed side would afford shelter from the biting blasts.

That Jesus should have employed 'shepherd' language on this occasion (26ff.) is perfectly credible. 'Shepherd' readings were common in the synagogues around Dedication time, as Ezek. 34 (the most important Old Testament passage for understanding John 10) was one of the Dedication *haphtaroth*. No topic would have been more natural on Jesus' lips at Hanukkah than one which the people had recently heard in their synagogues.

The controversy itself handles two issues—Jesus as Messiah (24) and Jesus as God or Son of God (33). Now these are precisely the questions which, according to the synoptics, arose at Jesus' trial before the Sanhedrin—indeed v. 24 is almost verbally identical with Luke 22.67-68. To be sure, St John has scattered these charges through a longer final ministry in Jerusalem; but such a longer ministry, we have already argued, is extremely probable, and John may be giving us the true picture of what actually happened, for the trial in the synoptics sounds like the repetition of older charges.

Jesus' appeal to his 'works' (25, 37f.), though the wording is Johannine, reminds us of the like reply he made to John the Baptist when he asked a similar question about his Messiahship (Matt. 11.2-6; Luke 7.18-23).

The argument from scripture in vv. 34-36 is, we have already suggested, not likely to have been invented. Not only is this rabbinical-sounding riposte credible, but the use of the verb 'consecrated' (*hēgiasen*) in v. 36 was probably inspired by Num. 7.1 (Moses' consecration of the tabernacle) which was a *seder* for the festival of Dedication.

Finally, the whole is rounded off with what is probably a fragment of itinerary material from tradition (40).

Despite, therefore, clear evidence that John has put his own stamp on the controversy, we believe that both its setting and basic content are traditional and authentic.

We cannot close our discussion of the Johannine discourses without a reference, however brief, to the 'sacred farewells' of Jesus.

Perhaps the most striking difference between the fourth and the first three gospels lies in John's record of what passed between Jesus and his disciples on the night of the Last Supper. If we had only the synoptics, we should know little beyond the fact that they held the Last Supper together and that Jesus predicted his betrayal and Peter's denial. True, St Luke, who evidently possessed a special Passion source, goes somewhat beyond Mark and Matthew, but he does not greatly add to our knowledge. John, however, undertakes to lift the veil and let us hear Jesus comforting and instructing his disciples in the shadow of the Cross. Lacking here, as we do, synoptic equivalents for comparison, can we believe that Jesus spoke to his disciples substantially as John says he did? We shall, of course, expect to find that all has passed through the alembic of John's own mind and will accordingly bear the stamp of his style and reflect his Christian experience. But if not verbally, is it substantially trustworthy?

Let us put forward three general considerations:

First: In our previous discussion we have found evidence enough that John, though he may interpret, does not arbitrarily invent: rather he builds and expands on tradition. The likelihood is that he does the same thing here. In other words he depends on a tradition of what Jesus actually said in the Upper Room.

Second: It is certain that the events of that last night together must have left an indelible impression on the memories of all who were present in the Upper Room. The Beloved Disciple, who was probably John, son of Zebedee, was there, and he is probably the source for the historical tradition which lies behind the fourth gospel.[20] Must not his memory underlie the fourth gospel's record of what was said on that never-to-be-forgotten evening?

Third: It was a saying of Burkitt's[21] that, though the words of Jesus in the fourth gospel are couched in the peculiar dialect of the evangelist, 'the ideas are the ideas which animated the sayings in the synoptic gospels'. Apply this dictum to the first part of the farewell discourses in John (13.31-14.31). What are its themes? They are the coming departure of Jesus, Peter's denial, the parable of the heavenly home, the commandment of love, Jesus the only true way to the Father, obedience the test of true allegiance to himself, the promise of the Paraclete, 'I will come to you'.

It is surely not incredible that on that last night together Jesus should have spoken to his disciples of his death and its sequel, comforted them with an assurance of a Father's house with many rooms, reiterated the law of love, insisted on obedience to his commands as the true test of their continuing allegiance, and promised them the aid of the Holy Spirit.

These are general, but not unimportant, considerations bearing on this problem of untrustworthiness. But it can be approached in yet another way.

The farewell discourses contain predictions by Jesus about his own death and victory over it and about the future of the disciples in the world. Now, though the synoptics preserve no similar 'farewells', elsewhere they do preserve teachings of Jesus about the future—we think particularly of the Mission Charge in Matt. 10 and the eschatological discourse in Mark 13. These synoptic predictions may be compared with those in John 14-16, in order to discover what our Lord had to say about his own and the disciples' future beyond the Cross. Happily this difficult task has been accomplished for us by C. H. Dodd, and—though not all scholars will agree with him—his conclusion is well worth pondering: [22]

> John is here (in the farewell discourses) reaching back to a very early form of tradition indeed, and making it the point of departure for his profound theological interpretation; and, further, the oracular sayings which he reports (i.e. about Christ's death and its sequel) have good claim to represent authentically, in substance if not verbally, what Jesus actually said to his disciples.

In other words, the revelation contained in the farewell discourses may well come authentically from Jesus, even if today it is across the soul of John that we behold it. Is not this most of what 'the parish priest' and 'the straightforward layman' could desire?

Our argument for the substantial authenticity of the sayings of Jesus in St John, which has been cumulative, ought to show how far modern scholarship has departed from the judgment of Renan. By way of epilogue, let us take up again a question raised earlier —that of the Aramaic element in John's gospel. Do the Johannine sayings of Jesus, despite evidence of 'targumizing', suggest underlying Aramaic originals? Bultmann has argued that behind the gospel there lies a *Reden-quelle*—i.e. some sort of Johannine Q. Likewise the late T. W. Manson[23] (basing himself on Burney's work) suggested that the Aramaisms mostly occur not in the narrative parts but in the discourses recorded by John. We may end by quoting the most recent and expert opinion on this question—that of Matthew Black: [24]

> It was Streeter who coined the phrase 'interpretative transformation' to describe the Johannine discourses. An inspired 'targumizing' of an Aramaic sayings tradition, early committed to a Greek form, is the most likely explanation of the Johannine speeches; but, in that case, it is no different in character from the literary process which gave us the Synoptic *verba Christi*. For the extent of this process of 'transformation' we must await the results of further study; but in the light of recent work it would appear to be becoming a rapidly diminishing area: the rabbinical character of the discourses and their predominantly poetical form certainly do not discourage the belief that much more of the *ipsissima verba* of Jesus may have been preserved in the fourth gospel— with John as inspired 'author'—than we have dared believe possible for many years.

NOTES

[1] *The Life of Jesus*, p. 15.
[2] *The Fourth Gospel*, p. 20.
[3] *The Poetry of our Lord*, chapter 2.

⁴ *Hypsoun* means (a) crucify and (b) exalt. The Aramaic *zᵉqap* means both 'crucify' and 'raise up'.

⁵ *H.T.F.G.*, pp. 322ff. Dodd follows M. Albertz in his *Die Synoptischen Streitgespräche* (1921).

⁶ *Encyclopaedia Biblica*, ii, col. 1881. They included Mark 10.18, 13.22, and 15.34.

⁷ F. C. Burkitt, *The Gospel History and its Transmission*, p. 240.

⁸ *Studies in Pharisaism and the Gospels*, I, p. 12.

⁹ I should myself argue that John 7.20-25 and 8.17-20 preserve a genuine tradition of how Jesus argued with his Jerusalem critics, with an appeal in both cases to the Jewish law.

¹⁰ *A Death in the Desert*.

¹¹ *The Son of Man*, p. 411.

¹² *The History of Primitive Christianity*, II, p. 793.

¹³ Another synoptic 'point' become a 'star' in John is the 'sentness' of Jesus. In the synoptics Jesus declares that God has 'sent' him to proclaim release to the captives (Luke 4.18); and, later, in sending out his 'apostles', assures them that to 'receive' him is to 'receive him that sent him' (Matt. 10.40; Luke 10.6). In St John 'he that sent me' (26 times) has become a name for God on every other page of the gospel, as the concept of Jesus as God's 'apostle' sounds through practically every discourse.

¹⁴ For the special problem raised by the 'eucharistic words' of vv. 51-58 see R. E. Brown, *A.B.S.J.*, *ad loc*.

¹⁵ E. C. Hoskyns, *The Fourth Gospel*, p. 288.

¹⁶ *Z.N.W.* 54-55, 1963-64, pp. 232-240.

¹⁷ In his *The New Testament and the Jewish Lectionaries* (1964) L. Morris has seriously damaged A. Guilding's main thesis in her *Fourth Gospel and Jewish Worship* (1960)—that the gospel is a book of sermons based on the Jewish synagogue lectionary. Yet it remains reasonably certain that in Christ's time there was a triennial cycle of *sedarim* (lections from the Law) in use in the synagogue—if not a fixed set of *haphtaroth* (lections from the prophets). For our purpose the chief point is the probability that the festival Discourses in John echo themes heard in the synagogues around festival season.

¹⁸ *John 6 and the Jewish Passover* (1959).

¹⁹ When in John 6.35, 45 and 47f. Jesus invites men to come to him as the Bread of Life, he is speaking *in persona sapientiae* (as he sometimes does in the synoptics). The bread of life, like the living water, represents Jesus and the divine revelation he brings. In the OT Wisdom literature (see, for example, Prov. 9.5; Isa. 55.1, 3, 10f.; and Ecclus 24.21) the divine word and wisdom are often symbolized by bread or food.

²⁰ See next chapter.

²¹ *The Gospel History and its Transmission*, p. 237.

²² *H.T.F.G.*, p. 420.

²³ *Studies in the Gospels and Epistles*, p. 115.

²⁴ *An Aramaic Approach to the Gospels and Acts*³ (1967), p. 151.

10

The Authority and Abiding Relevance
of John's Gospel

I

I N our previous chapters we have had little to say directly on the stock questions of place of origin, date and authorship. Now, however, before we discuss the abiding worth of the gospel, we must touch on these questions, however briefly.

On the question of provenance we have nothing new to propose. The ancient evidence (Irenaeus and Polycrates) points to Ephesus. A modern suggestion that Alexandria may have been the gospel's place of origin has not found much favour. More is to be said for the claim of Antioch, since the Epistles of Ignatius bishop of Antioch and the Gospel of Matthew (thought to have been written in Antioch) show some theological affinities with the Gospel of John and the First Epistle. But these are hardly sufficient to warrant us rejecting the testimony of tradition, and Ephesus therefore remains, in racing parlance, much the best bet.

When was the gospel written? The discovery in 1920 of the Rylands Fragment of the fourth gospel proves that the gospel was circulating in Egypt around A.D. 130 and must—if we allow a generation for the book to travel from Ephesus and become known in Egypt—have been written not later than A.D. 100. How early we date it depends on whether we think 'John' knew the gospels of Mark and Luke. If he knew them both (Streeter's position) the date can hardly be earlier than A.D. 90. If he did not know them— and this has been a central contention of this book—we may date John's gospel at least as early as A.D. 80. Of course the tradition preserved in it must be a good deal earlier—as early as that underlying the synoptics.

So we come to the question of authorship. What (or who) is the source of the ancient Palestinian tradition which is preserved in the gospel? The Bishop of Woolwich has suggested that one consequence of the new stress on the historicity of the gospel is that we now seek to trace its tradition back 'not through the memory of one old man but through the ongoing life of a community'. But can we thus lightly break the traditional link between the gospel and the 'one old man'? Could the early and excellent tradition conceivably go back to John the Apostle?

Any satisfactory solution to the problem of authorship must do justice to three things—the ancient evidence, the witness of the gospel itself, and the findings of modern scholarship.

(i) Without deploying again all the ancient testimony (see the commentaries of Bernard and Barrett) we may say that the testimony of Irenaeus remains, after all criticism, impressive. Irenaeus declared that 'John the disciple of the Lord, who leaned on his breast, himself issued the gospel while dwelling in Ephesus'. This testimony is supported by the Muratorian Canon (Hippolytus?), Polycrates of Ephesus, Clement of Alexandria, Tertullian and Origen. Beyond doubt Irenaeus believed the gospel to be the work of John the Apostle. What makes his testimony so strong is the fact that as a boy he had heard Polycarp tell of his intercourse with John the disciple of the Lord. Is there any cogent evidence to the contrary? Certainly not the very late and highly dubious evidence that John the Apostle was martyred early.[1] The fact that Irenaeus attributed all *five* Johannine books to the Apostle may be held to weaken his testimony a little. So may the fact that at the end of the second century a group of heretics nicknamed the *Alogi* and the Roman presbyter Gaius rejected the gospel; but their rejection may be explained by the gospel's popularity with the Gnostics and its doctrine of the Logos. Take it all in all, Irenaeus' ascription of the gospel to John the Apostle cannot lightly be dismissed. It is worth adding that the Muratorian Canon and Clement of Alexandria associate others with the Apostle in the inception of the gospel. (Cf. John 21.24, where others set their seal to the truth of what is written.)

(ii) Consider next the witness of the gospel itself. In the previous chapters we have shown (*a*) that the author's Greek has an unmistakable Semitic idiom; (*b*) that the gospel's basic background is Jewish; (*c*) that its accurate topography suggests one who had known southern Palestine at first-hand; and (*d*) that the writer had access to ancient tradition, independent of the synoptics, probably existing originally in Aramaic and reflecting the Palestinian political scene before the outbreak of the Jewish War. These features certainly encourage us to pursue a possible link with the 'one old man' of tradition. But they do not stand alone. The gospel claims on this point and that to depend on eye-witness tradition.

Thus in 19.34f., after the evangelist has related the flow of blood and water from Christ's side, he adds: 'This is vouched for by the evidence of an eye-witness, whose evidence is to be trusted' (NEB). If we ask who this eye-witness is, 'the beloved disciple', mentioned eight verses earlier as present at the foot of the Cross, seems the likeliest person.

Again in 21.24, which sounds like the certificate of the Ephesian elders, we read: 'It is this same disciple (the beloved disciple) who attests what here has been written. It is in fact he who wrote it,[2] and we know that his testimony is true' (NEB).

To the question, Who was the beloved disciple? there have been several answers: Lazarus, John Mark, the Rich Young Ruler, etc. But there is only one answer which meets the obvious requirements: John, son of Zebedee. (1) Except in John 21.2 the son of Zebedee is not mentioned in the gospel. Now John was one of Jesus' inner circle. The gospel's failure to mention him is very odd indeed—unless in fact his name is hidden in the title 'the disciple whom Jesus loved'. (2) The close association with Peter in the description of the Beloved Disciple (13.23f., 20.2, 21.7, 20-24) fits nobody so well as John. In the synoptics Peter and John appear regularly together, as they are paired in Acts 3-4. (3) Only the Twelve were present at the Last Supper (Mark 14.17). Among these the three closest to Jesus were Peter, James and John. John 13.23f. clearly distinguishes Peter from the Beloved Disciple; and according to Acts 12.2 James had been killed by King Herod in the early forties. So we are left with John.

(iii) The traditional solution of the gospel's authorship is tempting. If we cannot accept it, the reason is not simply the unlikelihood that John would have called himself 'the Beloved Disciple'. Nor is it only that we should have expected the son of Zebedee to quote the sayings of Jesus in a form more closely resembling what we find in the synoptics. There is another consideration.

Modern scholars have shown that the gospel received a measure of editing and revision before it was given to the world. (Here we may recall that the Muratorian Canon speaks of his fellow-disciples helping John with the *revision* of his gospel—*recognoscere* is the Latin verb used.) We think of the correcting parenthesis in 4.2 or of the statement in 21.24 referring to the Beloved Disciple in the third person. But this is not all. The Prologue, possibly a pre-Johannine Christian hymn, was probably added after the main body of the gospel had been written.[3] The proper setting for 'the eucharistic words' of John 6.51-58 would seem to be the Last Supper; but they now stand in the Galilean discourse about the Bread of Life.[4] And chapter 21, commonly called the Appendix to the Fourth Gospel, was probably added later, as its verse 24 reads like the certificate of the elders of the Church at Ephesus.

Accordingly a mediate solution of the problem of authorship is that which best fits all the facts.

First: There is nothing unscientific or improbable in holding that John the Apostle was the source of the ancient tradition behind the gospel. In the sense that he is the 'authority' behind the gospel, he is its 'author'. (For us 'author' and 'writer' mean the same thing. In the Bible, however, if a writer has disciples who carry on his work, even after his death, their work may be ascribed to him as 'author'. An excellent example is the book of Isaiah.)

Second: The actual evangelist was a close disciple of the apostle, and himself a man of deep spiritual insight. This man was almost certainly the Elder to whom we owe the Johannine Epistles. He may have been John the Elder of whom Papias writes. He, or some of his colleagues, were responsible for the editing and revision of the gospel.

If we are right in thinking that the authority of John the Apostle stands behind the gospel, we may compare his relation to the actual evangelist with that which Papias said existed between Peter and Mark.[5]

We have shown how deeply rooted the gospel is in ancient tradition, and argued that the tradition, though interpreted in the profoundest fashion, probably goes back to John the Apostle as *fons et origo*. In a word, we have sought to maintain the essential apostolicity of the gospel. It remains, by way of epilogue, to try to bring out the abiding value and relevance of the book.

Why does this gospel, in spite of all changes wrought by the passage of nineteen centuries, continue to 'speak to the condition' of so many Christians, high and humble, learned and unlearned?

We suggest that there are at least three reasons: (1) It is the Gospel of Life; (2) it exposes the person and work of Christ in depth; and (3) it presents the challenge of Christ and the Gospel in an existential way.

II

'Tis life whereof our nerves are scant,
Oh life, not death, for which we pant,
More life, and fuller that I want.

The poet's *cri de coeur* is supported by students of the science of religion who tell us that all religion is a 'prayer for life'. In St John's view God has answered that prayer in Christ. Salvation for him is life. Life is what the gospel offers the believer in Christ (3.16).

As a matter of mere statistics, 'life' occurs nineteen times in the fourth gospel, and seven times in I John; 'eternal life' seventeen times in the gospel, and six times in the epistle. The two are obviously interchangeable. What does St John mean by 'life' or 'eternal life'?

In the synoptics the Kingdom of God is the central theme. But if Jesus in the synoptics spoke oftener of the Kingdom he also spoke there of 'life' and 'eternal life', as the concordance will show. And when you study a passage like Mark 10.17-31 it becomes clear that to follow Jesus=to inherit eternal life=to enter the Kingdom =to be saved. Indeed, we should not be so very far from the truth if, in reading the New Testament, we made the equations: To 'be in the Kingdom of God'=to 'be in Christ'='to have eternal life'.

Why did St John prefer 'Life' to 'the Kingdom of God'? Possibly because 'the Kingdom of God' was a thoroughly Jewish concept not likely to be readily intelligible to the wider spiritual constituency to which he wanted to appeal. But all men, whether Jews or Gentiles, would be interested in a gospel which spoke of 'life'.

Yet John's concept of eternal life is Jewish in origin. It has its roots in the Old Testament doctrine of the living God with whom 'is the fountain of life'. You will find the phrase in Daniel 12.2, the Psalms of Solomon, the writings of the rabbis and the Dead Sea scrolls.[6] 'Eternal life' should be distinguished from 'everlasting life' which is merely durational, life that, like Tennyson's brook, merely goes on for ever. Rather is it a qualitative term, denoting the life that is life indeed, life lived in the presence and favour of

God, life, which, because it is God's own life, can never die. Again, 'eternal life' is, strictly, the life of the Age (to Come) and therefore, for the Jew, belongs to the future. What, however, is remarkable in John is that this future boon has become a present reality, something to be experienced here and now. And if we ask what has made the difference, the short answer is the saving act of God, which we summarily call 'the Fact of Christ'.

With these few words of explanation we may now turn to the Gospel of John—and to the First Epistle, when it makes the point more clearly.

Again and again John uses the word 'life' for the new quality of life made possible by Christ's coming and the advent of the Spirit. We hear of 'life' first in the Prologue—'in him was life' it is written of the pre-incarnate Logos—and we hear it again in what may originally have been the last word of the gospel (20.31). And in between this prelude and this coda, 'life' is John's dominant theme. Whether it is God, or Christ, or the Spirit, 'living' or 'life-giving' may be predicted of each. Pre-eminently of course it is Christ, as God's mediator and messenger, who is the Life-giver. The purpose of his coming is that men 'may have life and have it more abundantly' (10.10). To Nicodemus and the Woman of Samaria eternal life is the gift he has to offer. 'You will not come to me that you may have life,' he chides the scripture-searching Jews (5.40). To the multitude in Galilee, at what we may call 'the Galilean Lord's Supper', he claims to be 'the bread of life', the bread of the Messianic Age (6.48). 'I am the resurrection and the life,' he tells the sorrowing Martha (11.25). 'I am the way, and the truth, and the life,' he assures his disciples in the Upper Room, 'because I live, you will live also' (14.6, 19). And this life-giving ministry climaxes in the Cross and Resurrection whereby his mission is universalized and life made available for all who believe in him. (Similarly, the true sub-title of his first epistle, is, as Law said, 'the Tests of Life', since the letter is a series of tests, or criteria for enabling men to know whether they have eternal life.)

In John, therefore, the main stress falls on 'realized eschatology' —on eternal life as a present possibility, the life of the Age to Come available, through faith in Christ, here and now. This does not mean that St John excludes the doctrine of a future consummation, of a 'last day' and judgment, and a final state of the blessed (5.28f., 6.39f., 54, 14.1f., etc.). Yet though 'final' eschatology has undoubtedly a place in John's thought, he does not accent it: through most of his references to eternal life rings the richness of present privilege, the necessity of deciding here and now for 'life' or 'death'.

Only once does he come near defining 'eternal life'—in 17.3: 'This is eternal life, that they know thee the only true God, and Jesus Christ whom thou hast sent.' For John eternal life is getting to know (*ginōskōsi:* present tense) the only real God through Jesus Christ, God's messenger to men. Such knowledge of God is not the acquisition of theological learning, neither is it mystical contemplation: it is a 'following on to know the Lord'—a personal communion with God through Christ, only to be perfected hereafter, since the unveiled glory of God is not for flesh and blood. 'All this (if we may re-apply a modern phrase) and heaven too' in a Father's house with many rooms (14.2).

Finally, St John regards this eternal life as something which affects the whole man, making him not merely a wiser but a better man, and manifesting itself above all in *agape*, that *agape* which is the grateful response in man to the divine *agape* whose crucial act 'was actually performed in history, on an April day about A.D. 30, at a supper table in Jerusalem, in a garden across the Kidron valley, in the headquarters of Pontius Pilate, and on a Roman cross at Golgotha'.[7] Christian love, therefore, for John is a sacrificial love like Christ's who loved his own utterly and to the end (13.1). It is the mark of his true disciples in the world (13.35), and the sign that believers 'have passed from death to life' (I John 3.14).

In his emphasis on Christianity as new, divine life, St John, like any good evangelist, doubtless had in view potential readers of his gospel—not Jews of the Diaspora only (as some modern scholars have thought) but that wider world of men in the first century, suffering from spiritual 'loss of nerve', incredulous of the old faiths, and hungry for a word of life in a world of death. If we would appreciate the goodness of his 'good news', we have only to consider contemporary rabbis or Stoics. The rabbis were earnest, scrupulous, high-minded men, zealous for God's honour and gravely concerned for godliness and the good life. So, too, were the Stoics, as we see them at their best in Seneca and Epictetus, with their belief in Divine Reason at the heart of things, their ideals of human brotherhood, and what Carlyle called 'their everlasting clatter about virtue'. But for all their zeal and earnestness, neither in the

rabbis nor in the Stoics was there 'any kick, any joy'. All was dull
as ditchwater. What did the Christians have, as witness the writings of St John, which neither rabbi nor Stoic had? T. W. Manson[8]
answers: 'A passionate devotion'—a devotion to a living Lord and
a call to reproduce in their own lives the new divine life that was
in him. In their faith and Christian experience they had an aware-
ness of 'life that was eternal, continually creative, continually
spending itself in love yet never diminished, the kind of life that
age does not weary or the years condemn'.

Such was the secret of the appeal of John's gospel towards the
end of the first century. Is it not even so still?

> It is the teaching of the New Testament, [wrote David S. Cairns][9] that
> there is nothing essential in the spiritual splendour of early Christianity
> which may not return, and is not meant to return. If the Christian
> Church today is not living on the ancient levels, it is not because God's
> gift of life has been withdrawn: it is because men will not appropriate
> and use the gift. The fountains of life in God have been opened once
> for all, and somewhere far above the low valley along which humanity
> is toiling today with weary and bleeding feet, the fountains of life are
> still springing in the sun.

These words were written during the First World War, but they
have not lost their relevance. To a war-torn and sin-sick world,
prone to lapse into nihilism or atheism, the gospel penned at
Ephesus nineteen hundred years ago still comes with its promise
of life through a Christ who is perennially the same. To have part
in that divine life of his through faith, and, while standing in the
midst of history, to be comprehended in eternal salvation through
him who calls himself 'the life' and 'the way' to life, is to be a
Christian and to have life eternal.

III

A second secret of the enduring worth of the fourth gospel is that
it depicts the person and work of Christ in depth.

In our time we have seen a growing *rapprochement* between the
fourth evangelist and the first three. Once it was almost an axiom
that you went to the synoptics for the Jesus of history, to John's
gospel for the Christ of faith. This sharp line-up of the first three
against the fourth gospel can no longer be justified. The old
assumption was that the synoptics were themselves histories, and
that John, if he were to be historical, must agree with them. Now,
thanks largely to the form critics, we know that none of the gospels

is history or biography in the strict sense of these terms. The object of the evangelists was to provide evangelical testimony, not scientific history (in the nineteenth century sense of recovering 'the bare facts' *sans* interpretation) or biography (in the sense of 'Boswellizing' Jesus). This does not mean that the gospels do not contain history—a book can be historical without being a history or a biography. It is all a question of the principle of organization and arrangement.

The tradition behind the synoptics, scholars now agree, is that of the preaching (*kērygma*) and teaching (*didachē*) of the primitive church. But because it rests back on the testimony of those who (in Luke's phrase) 'were from the beginning eye-witnesses and ministers of the Word', it is historical. The writers of the synoptics accepted the *kērygma* of the apostles and fitted into that framework the works and words of Jesus known to them, sometimes without clear chronological guidance. In other words, they arranged their materials on a *theological* rather than on a biographical principle. Each selected his materials according to the message he sought to convey. In a word, each was a theologian. Now in such a company of theologians St John seems perfectly in place, even if he still remains the theologian *par excellence* among them. But, as we have been emphasizing all along, he was not theologizing *in vacuo*—at his disposal he had an early and independent tradition which, going back to John the Apostle, at some points overlapped the synoptic tradition, but at others broke new ground.

The difference, therefore, between St John and the synoptists is a difference not of kind but of degree, a difference in depth. This, of course, is the position that has always been taken by the best British scholars from Westcott and Scott Holland to Hoskyns and Dodd.

One can maintain this thesis in many different ways. We have, for example, already argued that in the matter of miracles the difference is one of emphasis, not of kind.

Even in the synoptics, where they are called 'mighty works' and form part of Jesus' proclamation of God's saving sovereignty, the miracles are signs to those who, by piercing the mystery of Jesus' incognito, can see them as *Gesta Christi*. *Per contra*, St John expressly labels them as 'signs' which show God's (or Christ's) 'glory'—his saving presence in action. John's attitude to miracles is not really different from the synoptic one, for the signs of the fourth gospel also are to be understood only by those who have faith—the *doxa* of Jesus is veiled except from the eyes which have been opened to the true Light. But for John the theology of the miracles is a paramount concern. A 'sign', like the Old Testament *ōth*, is a significant act which conveys a deeper meaning than the actual happening; and it is part of John's deliberate purpose to draw out the profounder theological significance, so that men may see in the 'works' of Jesus the saving presence of God in action.

Consider next how the fourth gospel presents in depth Jesus' judgment on men. 'For judgment I came into this world,' says Jesus (3.19); and St John represents the whole historical ministry of Jesus as the judgment of men—or, rather, a self-judgment, since men judge themselves by their response to the challenge of Jesus, the incarnate Purpose (or Word) of God.

But if we will but ponder the matter, this is what also happens in the synoptic story of the Ministry. Whether it is the Rich Young Ruler or the three candidates for discipleship (Luke 9.57-62), men are judged by Jesus, or rather, by rejecting Jesus and the claims of the Kingdom, they reject themselves. So it is also in the Woes on Chorazin and Bethsaida in whose midst 'the mighty works' of the Kingdom had apparently been performed all in vain (Luke 10.13-15). Here, to be sure, the venue is Doomsday; but in fact the meaning is that, by rejecting Jesus and the Kingdom, his Galilean contemporaries have passed sentence on themselves. The same principle of judgment is enunciated when Jesus sends out his 'missionaries'. They are to proclaim the presence and claims of the Kingdom, and if men reject their message, they are to make it clear that the verdict has been already passed, by performing a symbolic action (Luke 10.9-12).

St John, therefore, elucidates in theological depth what was in fact happening when Jesus confronted his contemporaries with the challenge of the Kingdom, and this whole concept of Jesus as judge of men is summed up in the Upper Room, retrospectively and with solemn finality, 'If I had not come and *spoken* . . . if I had not *done* among them the works which no one else did, they would not be guilty of sin' (15.22-24). It is a judgment of both words and works.

Take, as a third illustration, John's doctrine of the Advocate-Spirit. In John 14-16 five 'paraclete' sayings describe the character and functions of the Holy Spirit who will be Christ's *Alter Ego* (not so much supplying his absence as accomplishing his presence) after he has returned to the Father by way of the Cross. This 'Spirit of truth' will be at once the disciples' Teacher, Christ's Witness-bearer, and the World's Accuser,[10] completing the revelation he has brought, and guiding his followers into all truth.

Similar sayings about the Holy Spirit in the Synoptics are few—cf. Mark 13.11; Luke 12.8-12; Matt. 10.20—yet they are enough to show that in the last stages of the training of the Twelve Jesus prepared them for a time when, no longer depending on his physical presence, they would be enabled to witness to him through the Holy Spirit, the Spirit of the Father. (Nor, in the light of all the evidence that John had access to independent tradition about the works and words of Jesus, is it at all unlikely that he knew of a fuller teaching of Jesus concerning the Spirit than the paucity of synoptic sayings would suggest.) No doubt, as we now have them, the five 'paraclete' sayings reflect the Christian experience of the evangelist and the Church; yet if they go beyond the *ipsissima verba* of Jesus, they do but spell out in richer language that teaching about the Spirit as the disciples' advocate found on Jesus' lips in the synoptics. Once again John has elucidated in depth.

By three examples we have tried to show that the fourth gospel, so far from being at variance with the first three, draws out in theological depth what is implicit in the first three. Some may grant all this and yet contend that there remain two crucial issues —eschatology and Christology—which show that, for all our talk of *rapprochement*, there still remains a wide gulf between John and the synoptics. Can we really maintain (they will say) that in these two theological areas what John has done is to see through to its depth what is implicit in the synoptic record of Jesus' words and works?

Take the matter of eschatology first. In the synoptics, as scholars have long recognized, we find an increasing tendency to accentu-ate the apocalyptic element in Jesus' teaching, with (if the phrase is permissible) St Matthew the chief sinner in this respect. On the other hand, what we find in John is strong stress on 'realized eschatology', without, however, the complete exclusion of the future note ('final' eschatology)—witness his repeated references to 'the last day' in 6.39-54.

Formerly, when everybody thought that John knew the synoptics, it was natural to argue that John was deliberately toning
down the apocalyptic note he found in them. Now, though admit-
tedly not all scholars will agree, we may plausibly hold that John
preserves a tradition of Jesus' eschatological teaching which has
not been apocalypticized, a tradition which more truly reflects the
mind of Jesus as we know it from Mark and Q.

We are here concerned with (a) the emphasis on 'inaugurated
eschatology' which marks the early chapters of John and (b) Jesus'
teaching about his death and its sequel—his 'predictive teaching'—
to be found in the farewell discourses. Examine the references to
the Kingdom in Mark and Q, and you will find that no less than
eighteen out of a total twenty-seven speak of the Kingdom as a
dawning or present reality—clear proof that for Jesus the Kingdom of God was in a real sense a *fait accompli* in his ministry,
whatever consummation was yet to come. Now, though John does
not make much use of 'Kingdom' language, it is this same stress on
'inaugurated eschatology' which is suggested by the formula 'The
hour cometh, *and now* is' which he sets on Jesus' lips in his colloquy
with the Samaritan Woman in chapter 4. This, it has been claimed,
is not only an acute theological definition but is 'essentially historical and probably represents the mind of Jesus as veraciously as
any formula could'.

On the other hand, if you compare the predictive teaching of
Jesus in the Upper Room Discourses, where Jesus is talking about
his death and its sequel, with what the synoptics record Jesus as
saying (a) about the disciples and their future (see Matt. 10 and
Mark 13) and (b) about his own death and what will follow it,
you may well come to the conclusion that John is here reaching
back to a very early form of the tradition and that the ora-
cular sayings he sets on Jesus' lips have a good claim—indeed
a better one than those in the synoptics—to represent in substance what Jesus said to his disciples before he went to the
Cross.[11]

Now consider the question of Christology. Is the Christ of St
John basically different from the Christ of the synoptics?

Certainly Mark and John had no idea that they were depicting
different Christs. As Mark's title indicates, his gospel was about
'Jesus Christ, the Son of God' (Mark 1.1). Similarly, John wrote to
foster saving faith in 'Jesus as the Christ, the Son of God' (John

20.31). Nevertheless, it has long been held that John here stands apart, that he gives us some kind of omniscient divine being who makes claims for himself far transcending those made by the synoptic Christ.

But is this a fair account of John's portrait of Jesus? Far more dominant in John, it seems to us, is the continual insistence on Jesus' *utter dependence*, at every point, on his heavenly Father. Ernest Davey[12] has shown how this feature runs right through the gospel. Now this emphasis on Jesus' dependence was surely never the invention of the early Church; it can only derive from tradition, must be a matter of history, not of dogmatic preconception. When we recognize this—and it is startlingly obvious once Davey has pointed it out—the alleged incongruity of the Johannine portrait with the synoptic one loses most of its force. Indeed we may then begin to perceive the truth in the statement of John Robinson:[13] 'In all the Gospels Jesus makes no claims for himself in his own right, and at the same time makes the most tremendous claims about what God is doing in and through him.' In so saying, Robinson wrongly (in our judgment) sets aside the evidence that Jesus claimed to be the Son, or the Son of God. But we may agree that in the synoptics the main stress is on what God is doing through Jesus.

The apostles (as witness the early speeches in Acts) took the same line. Their message was not, 'This man went about claiming that he was the Son of God.' It was: 'This Jesus whom you crucified God has made Lord and Christ.'

St John but deepens this paradox. In his gospel, says C. K. Barrett,[14] commenting on John 13.50, 'Jesus is not a figure of independent greatness: he is the Word of God, or he is nothing at all.' Again and again the Christ of St John says, 'If I claim anything for myself, do not believe me.' On the other hand, he just as surely declares, 'No one comes to the Father but by me.' If he does not claim to be God, he does claim to bring God, uniquely and decisively.

Our claim then is that John brings out the full implications of the common oral tradition about Jesus—brings out the person and work of Christ in depth, so that

> What first were guessed as points he now knew stars
> And named them in the Gospel he has writ.

IV

The third secret of the continuing relevance of John's gospel is
that it presents the challenge of Jesus to men existentially.

Existentialism is a modern word associated with Kierkegaard,
'the gloomy Dane in whom Hamlet was mastered by Christ'. In
his philosophy the individual and his place in the ultimate scheme
of things matter supremely, and all the stress falls on concern and
commitment. To think existentially is to think not as a spectator
of the ultimate issues of life and death but as one committed to a
decision on them: and it is existentialist teaching that knowledge
of God and his truth becomes ours only in the act of deciding for
it with 'all that in us is'.

But only the word is modern. The Bible is full of it, as are the
synoptic gospels. You will find it in Jesus' parables which summon
the hearer to 'see-judge-act', in what Jesus has to say about 'the
two ways' and the need to struggle, not to stroll, into the Kingdom,
in his call to choose between God and mammon, and so on. But it
is in John's gospel, with his way of expounding Christianity in
sharp and fateful antithesis—truth and falsehood, light and darkness, life and death,—that it comes out clearest.

John's existentialism takes many forms. It occurs in the most
famous verse he ever wrote—John 3.16. There the reader is confronted with the gospel's awful alternatives—life or death—and
warned that a man by rejecting God's gift in Christ may for ever
forfeit his chance of 'eternal life'. Existentialist, too, is that other
hardly less famous verse which declares that 'if any man will do
his will, he shall know of the doctrine, whether it is of God' (7.17).

A like existentialism rings through John's concepts of judgment
and faith.

Judgment, for John, is not so much a great end-of-the-world
assize as a present process and sifting. Even now God

> is sifting out the hearts of men
> Before his judgment seat

and men judge themselves by the attitude they take up to Christ
as the incarnate truth of God

> He who believes in him is not condemned,
> He who does not believe in him is condemned already (3.18).

So also John's concept of faith is existentialist. True belief is to 'turn away from the world and accept the life that Jesus gives and is'. Rightly, therefore, does Bultmann[15] call it 'transition into eschatological existence', since by the decision of faith a man passes from death to life.

Every reader of Bultmann knows how he sprinkles his pages with the word 'decision' (*Entscheidung*). In so doing he has put his finger on something which is basic to Christianity. T. W. Manson[16] puts it memorably and modernly thus:

> Against a cheap and easy optimism and an equally cheap and easy pessimism—the optimism of H. G. Wells and the pessimism of Aldous Huxley—stands the gospel which is neither rose-pink nor twilight-grey, but plain black and white. And one at least of its keys is Choose!

More than any of the evangelists St John has given expression to this challenge—a challenge that comes to every man and cannot be evaded, since silence implies dissent.

C. F. D. Moule[17] is making the same point when he argues that the fourth gospel is the most *individualistic* of the New Testament documents. This individualism (he says) is tied up with John's stress on realized eschatology, and the peculiar depth of the gospel lies largely in its analysis of the meaning of individual relations with God and Christ. Not only does it abound with individual encounters between Jesus and individuals, but from them spring sayings addressed to individuals, so that we almost get a one-by-one salvation. This is the reason why the gospel is so useful to men like evangelists and pastors who engage in personal dealings, for it 'is the gospel *par excellence* of the single soul in its approach to God'.

Nineteen centuries ago St John presented his Lord to the wider world in such existential ways. But the Christ who in the days of his flesh called me to decide for or against him as a matter of life or death, is no mere figure in an antique story. He is the risen and regnant Lord, our eternal Contemporary; the Spirit of God, who 'takes of the things of Christ and shows them unto us', makes him such; and it is not from Palestine only or the first century, but here and now that he is to be encountered and his challenge heard. If we may adapt Schweitzer's famous words, he comes to us still as he came to men and women in Galilee and Judea; he speaks the same word 'Follow me!' To the enquirer he says, 'If any man will to do his will, he shall know of the doctrine whether it is of God.' To those who long for assurance of eternal life he promises, 'Because I live, you shall live also.' And he sets us, his followers, to the tasks which he calls us to fulfil in this day and age, sure that, if we do so, we shall learn in the conflicts and sufferings which we will pass through in his service, who and what he is. Today it is still true that the disciple who loves his Lord and is loved by him will discern his face through the morning mist. And now, as of old, he confronts the defenders of his cause with the thrice-repeated challenge, 'Lovest thou me?'

NOTES

[1] J. H. Bernard, *St John*, pp. xxxvii-xlv.

[2] *Ho grapsas* may mean 'caused to be written'.

[3] See J. A. T. Robinson, *N.T.S.*, 1963, pp. 120-29.

[4] See R. E. Brown, *A.B.S.J.*, pp. 285ff.

[5] Our theory of authorship is basically that of Raymond Brown in his *Anchor Bible Commentary*, though we think that his hypothesis of *five* distinct stages in the gospel's composition is unduly speculative and complicated.

[6] See Dan. 12.2 (*hayye 'ōlam*, LXX. *zoē aiōnios*), Psalms of Solomon 3.16, I Q.S.4.7, and Dalman, *Words of Jesus*, pp. 156ff.

[7] C. H. Dodd, *I.F.G.*, p. 200.

[8] *On Paul and John*, p. 116.

[9] *The Reasonableness of the Christian Faith*, pp. 138f.

[10] We have already seen that down at Qumran they called the Holy Spirit 'the Spirit of truth' and spoke of his functions in a juridical way.

[11] See Dodd, *I.F.G.*, p. 447; *H.T.F.G.*, p. 420. The same essential view of Jesus' eschatology will be found in T. F. Glasson's *The Second Advent* and J. A. T. Robinson's *Jesus and His Coming*, Chapter 8.

[12] See his *The Jesus of St John* (1958).

[13] See his fine essay in *The Roads Converge*, p. 71, to which I am here indebted.

[14] *The Gospel according to St John*, p. 362.

[15] *The Theology of the New Testament*, II, p. 76.

[16] *On Paul and John*, p. 89.

[17] *Novum Testamentum*, Vol. V. Fasc 2/3 (1962).

BIBLIOGRAPHY

ABBOTT, E. A., *The Son of Man*, New York : Macmillan, 1909; Cambridge University Press, 1910.

ABRAHAMS, ISRAEL, *Studies in Pharisaism and the Gospels*, Cambridge University Press, 1924.

ALBERTZ, M., *Die Synoptischen Streitgespräche*, 1921.

ALLEGRO, J. M., *The Dead Sea Scrolls*, London : Penguin Books, 1959.

ARNOLD, MATTHEW, *God and the Bible*, 1875.

BARRETT, C. K., *The Gospel according to St John*, London : S.P.C.K.; New York : Macmillan, 1955.

BERNARD, J. H., *St John*. International Critical Commentaries. Edinburgh : T. and T. Clark, 1929.

BLACK, MATTHEW, *An Aramaic Approach to the Gospel and Acts*[3], Oxford University Press, 1967.

BORSCH, F. H., *The Son of Man in Myth and History*, London : SCM Press; Philadelphia : Westminster Press, 1967.

BROWN, R. E., *The Gospel according to St John*. Anchor Bible Commentary, New York : Doubleday, 1966.

New Testament Essays, Milwaukee : Bruce Publishing Co., 1965; London : Geoffrey Chapman, 1966.

BULTMANN, RUDOLF, *Das Evangelium des Johannes*, Göttingen, 1941.

Jesus and the Word, London : Collins, Fontana Books, 1962.

Theology of the New Testament, Vols. I and II. New York : Scribners; London : SCM Press, 1952-55.

BURKITT, F. C., *The Gospel History and its Transmission*, Edinburgh : T. and T. Clark, 1906.

BURNEY, C. F., *The Aramaic Origin of the Fourth Gospel*, Oxford University Press, 1922.

The Poetry of our Lord, Oxford University Press, 1925.

BURROWS, MILLAR, *The Dead Sea Scrolls*, London : Secker & Warburg, 1956.

CAIRNS, DAVID S., *The Reasonableness of the Christian Faith*, London: Hodder & Stoughton, 1918.

COLWELL, E. C., *The Greek of the Fourth Gospel*, University of Chicago Press, 1931.

CRANFIELD, C. E. B., *St Mark*, Cambridge University Press, 1959.

CROSS, F. L. (ed.), *The Gospels Reconsidered*, Oxford: Blackwell, 1960.

CROSS, F. M., *The Ancient Library of Qumran*, London: Duckworth, 1958.

DALMAN, GUSTAF, *The Words of Jesus*, Edinburgh: T. and T. Clark, 1909.

DAVEY, J. E., *The Jesus of St John*, London: Lutterworth Press, 1958.

DAVIES, W. D. and DAUBE, D. (eds.), *The Background of the New Testament and its Eschatology*, Cambridge University Press, 1954.

DODD, C. H., *According to the Scriptures*, London: Nisbet, 1952.
Historical Tradition in the Fourth Gospel, Cambridge University Press, 1963.
The Interpretation of the Fourth Gospel, Cambridge University Press, 1953.

FULLER, R. H., *Interpreting the Miracles*, London: SCM Press; Philadelphia: Westminster Press, 1963.

GARDNER-SMITH, P., *St John and the Synoptic Gospels*, Cambridge University Press, 1938.
The Roads Converge, London: E. Arnold, 1963.

GÄRTNER, B., *John 6 and the Jewish Passover*, 1959.

GLASSON, T. F., *Moses in the Fourth Gospel*, London: SCM Press, 1963.
The Second Advent, London: Epworth Press, 1963.

GOGUEL, M., *The Life of Jesus*, London: Allen and Unwin, 1933.

GUILDING, A., *The Fourth Gospel and Jewish Worship*, Oxford: Clarendon Press, 1960.

HIGGINS, A. J. B., *The Historicity of the Fourth Gospel*, London: Lutterworth Press, 1960.

HOLLAND, H. SCOTT, *The Fourth Gospel*, 1923.

HOSKYNS, E. C. and F. N. DAVEY, *The Fourth Gospel*, London: Faber, 1947.

HOWARD, W. F., *Christianity according to St John*, London: Duckworth, 1943.

JEREMIAS, J., *Die Wiederentdeckung von Bethesda*, Vandenhoeck und Ruprecht, 1949.

LIGHTFOOT, J. B., *Biblical Essays*, 1893.

MACGREGOR, G. H. C., *The Gospel of John*, Moffatt New Testament Commentaries, London: Hodder & Stoughton, 1928.

MANSON, T. W., *On Paul and John*, London: SCM Press, 1963.
The Servant-Messiah, Cambridge University Press, 1953.
Studies in the Gospels and Epistles, Manchester University Press, 1962.

MORRIS, L., *The New Testament and the Jewish Lectionaries*, London: Tyndale Press, 1964.

NOACK, BENT, *Zur Johanneischen Tradition*, København: Rosenkilde og Bagger, 1954.

PALEY, WILLIAM, *The Evidences of Christianity*, 1794.

PREISS, THEO, *Life in Christ*, London: SCM Press, 1954.

RENAN, E., *The Life of Jesus*, 1863.

RICHARDSON, ALAN, *History, Sacred and Profane*, London: SCM Press; Philadelphia: Westminster Press, 1964.

ROBINSON, J. A. T., *Jesus and His Coming*, London: SCM Press; Nashville: Abingdon, 1957.
Twelve New Testament Studies, London: SCM Press, 1962.

SANDAY, WILLIAM, *Outlines of the Life of Christ*, Edinburgh: T. and T. Clark, 1905.

SCHMIDT, K. L., *Der Rahmen der Geschichte Jesu*, 1919.

SCHWEIZER, EDUARD, *Ego Eimi²*, Göttingen: Vandenhoeck und Ruprecht, 1965.

SCOBIE, C., *John the Baptist*, London: SCM Press; Philadelphia: Fortress Press, 1964.

SMITH, C. W. F., *The Jesus of the Parables*, Philadelphia: Westminster Press, 1964.

STREETER, B. H., *The Four Gospels*, London: Macmillan, 1924.

TAYLOR, V., *The Gospel according to St Mark*, London: Macmillan, 1966.

WEISS, JOHANNES, *The History of Primitive Christianity*, London: Macmillan, 1937.

WESTCOTT, B. F., *The Gospel according to St John*, 1881 (London: James Clarke, 1958).

INDEX OF NAMES

INDEX OF BIBLICAL REFERENCES